Inspirational Images

David Leahy

ISBN-13: 978-0995663039
ISBN-10: 09956630

Introduction

These are 100 of the best images that I photographed whilst traveling the world (and some from closer to home). Some of them prompted words, an idea or a quote, so I took inspiration to add appropriate words to all of them. Enjoy.

See the Northern lights at least once

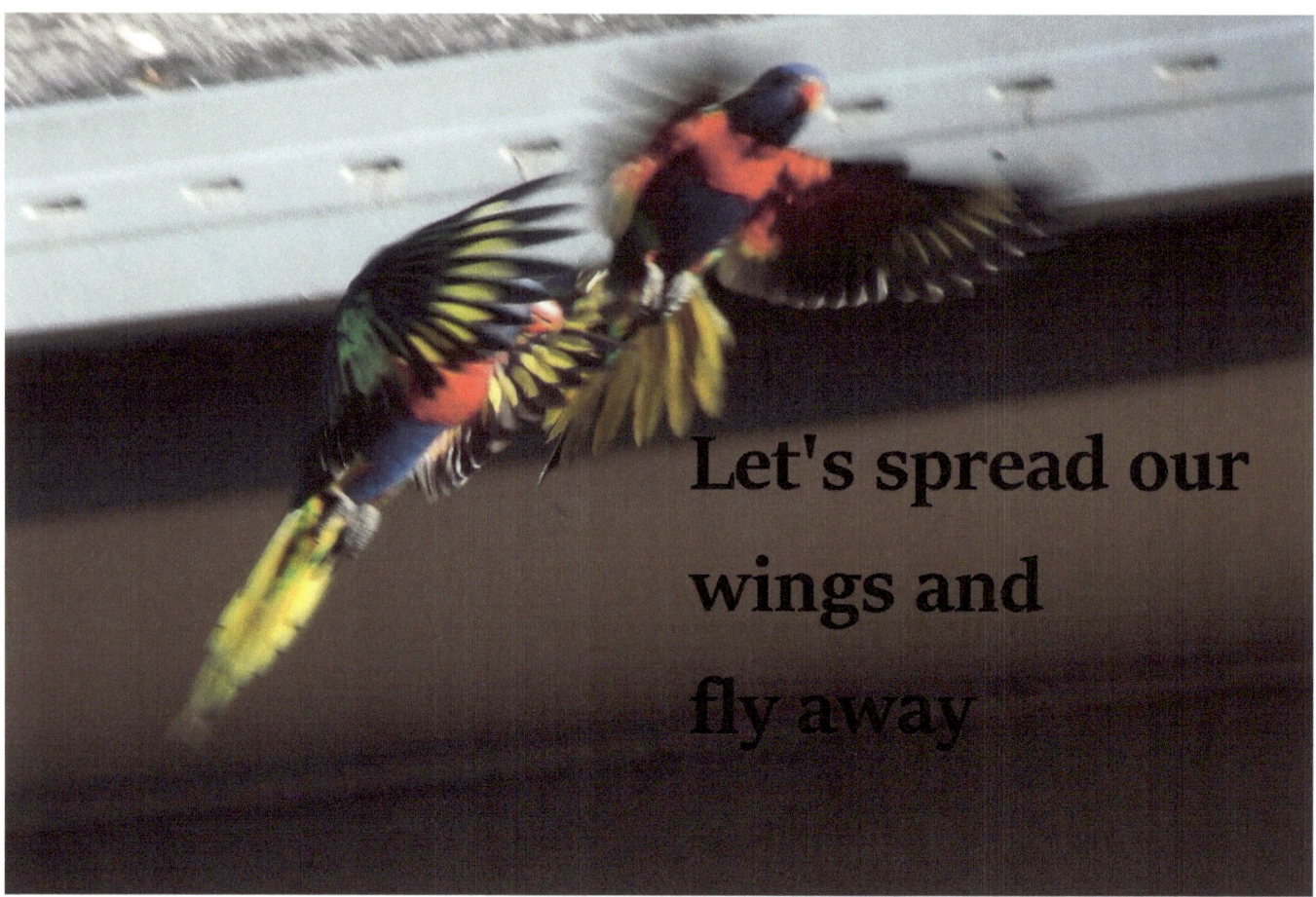

Let's spread our wings and fly away

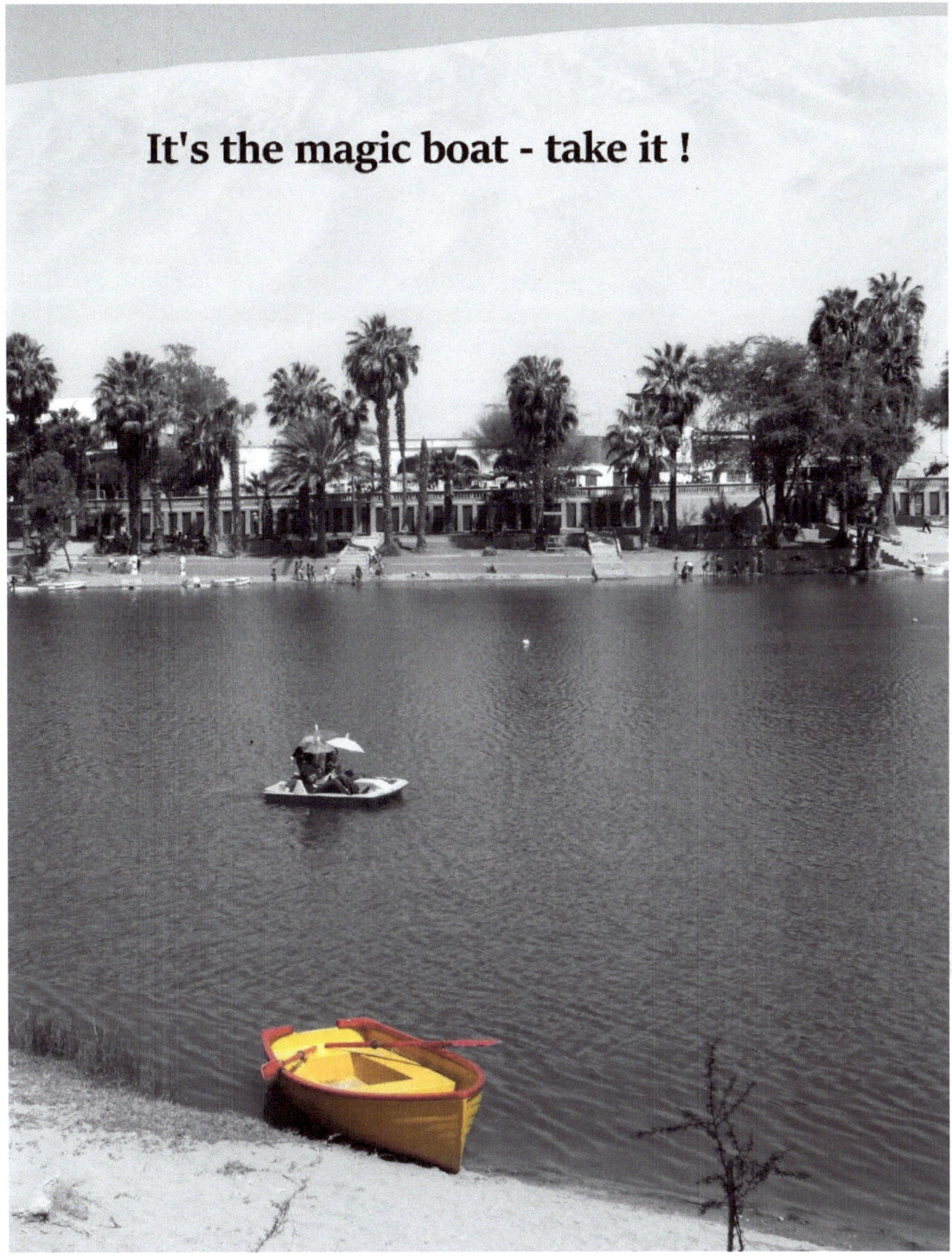

Symmetry

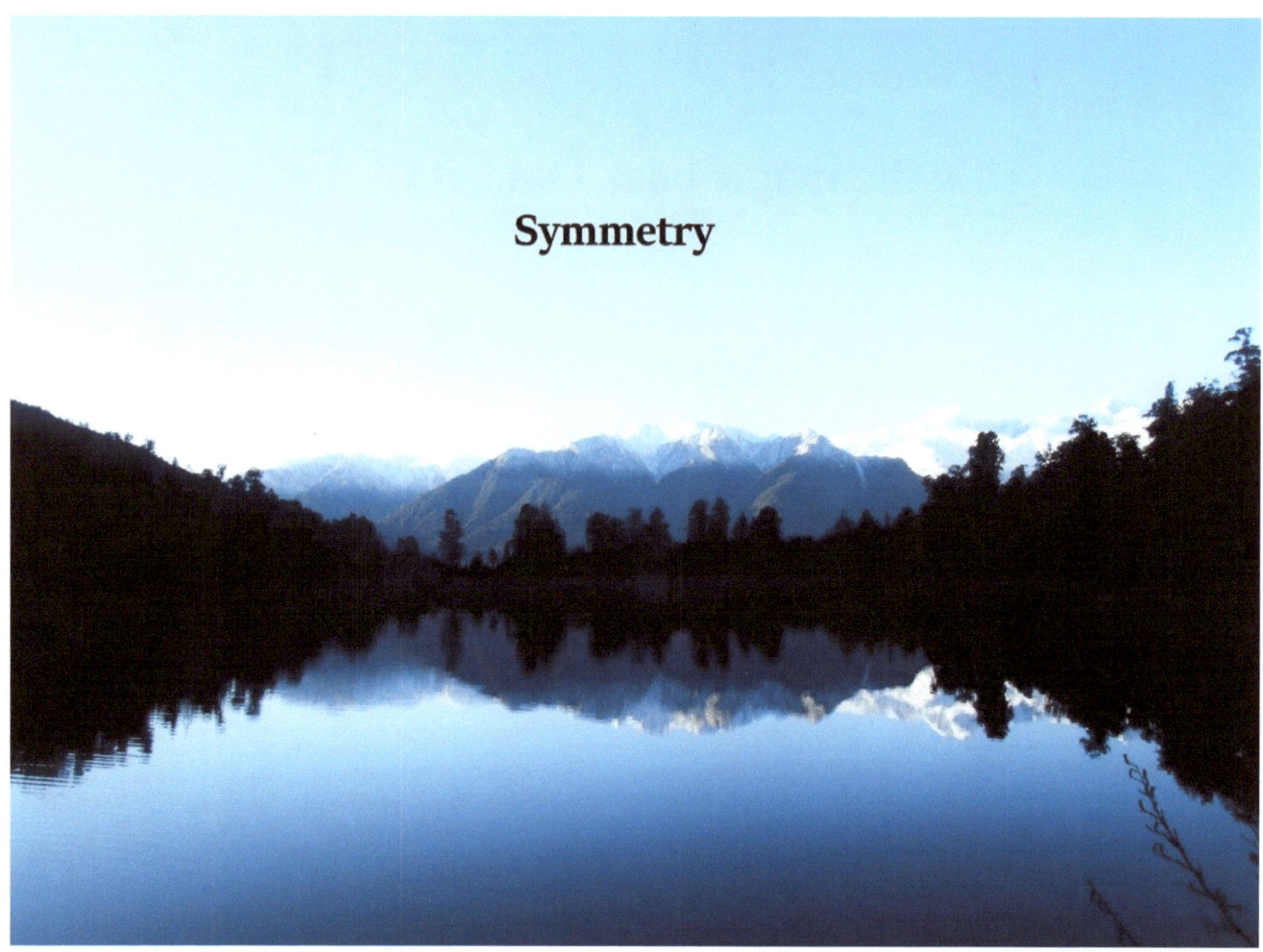

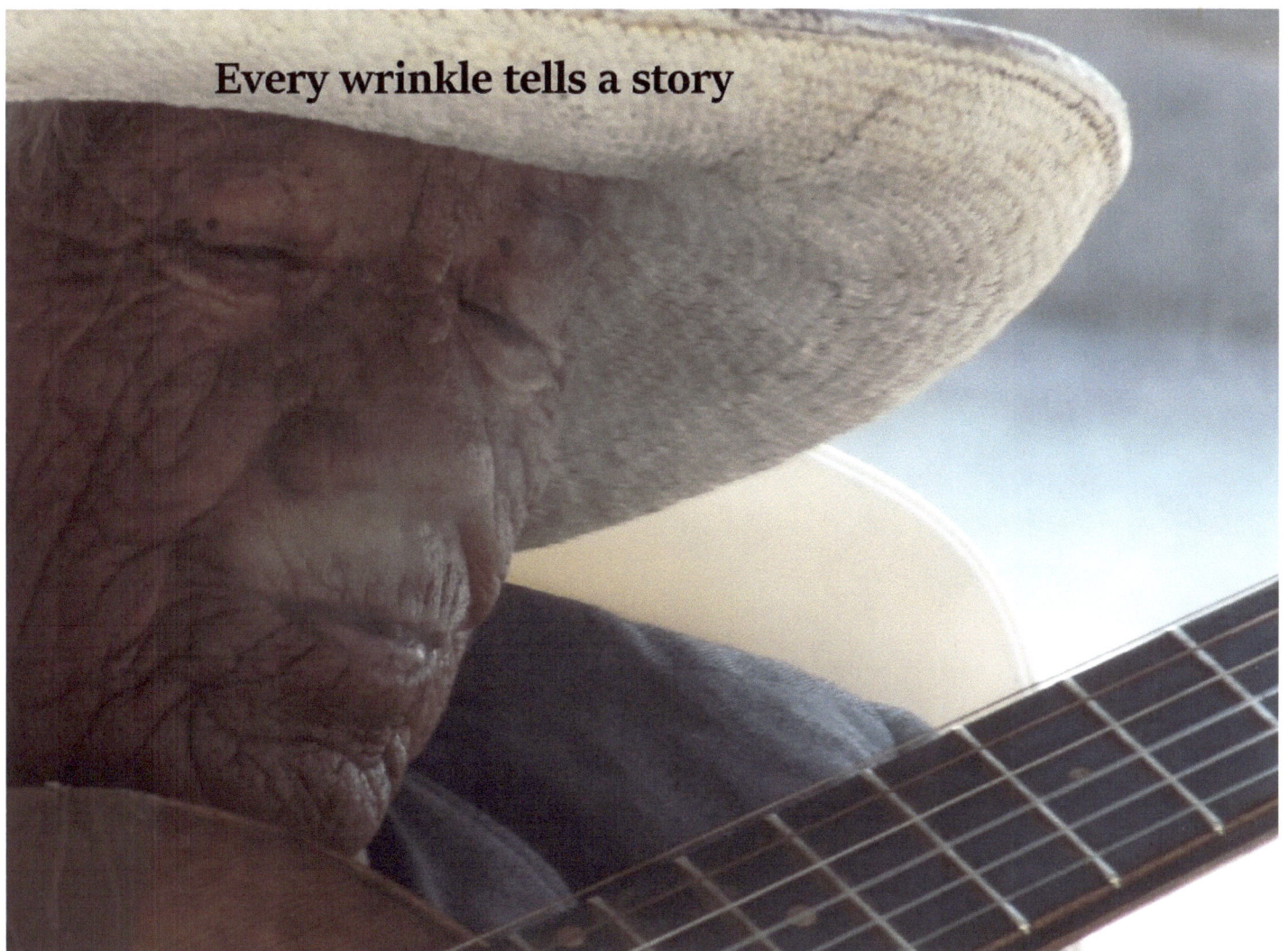

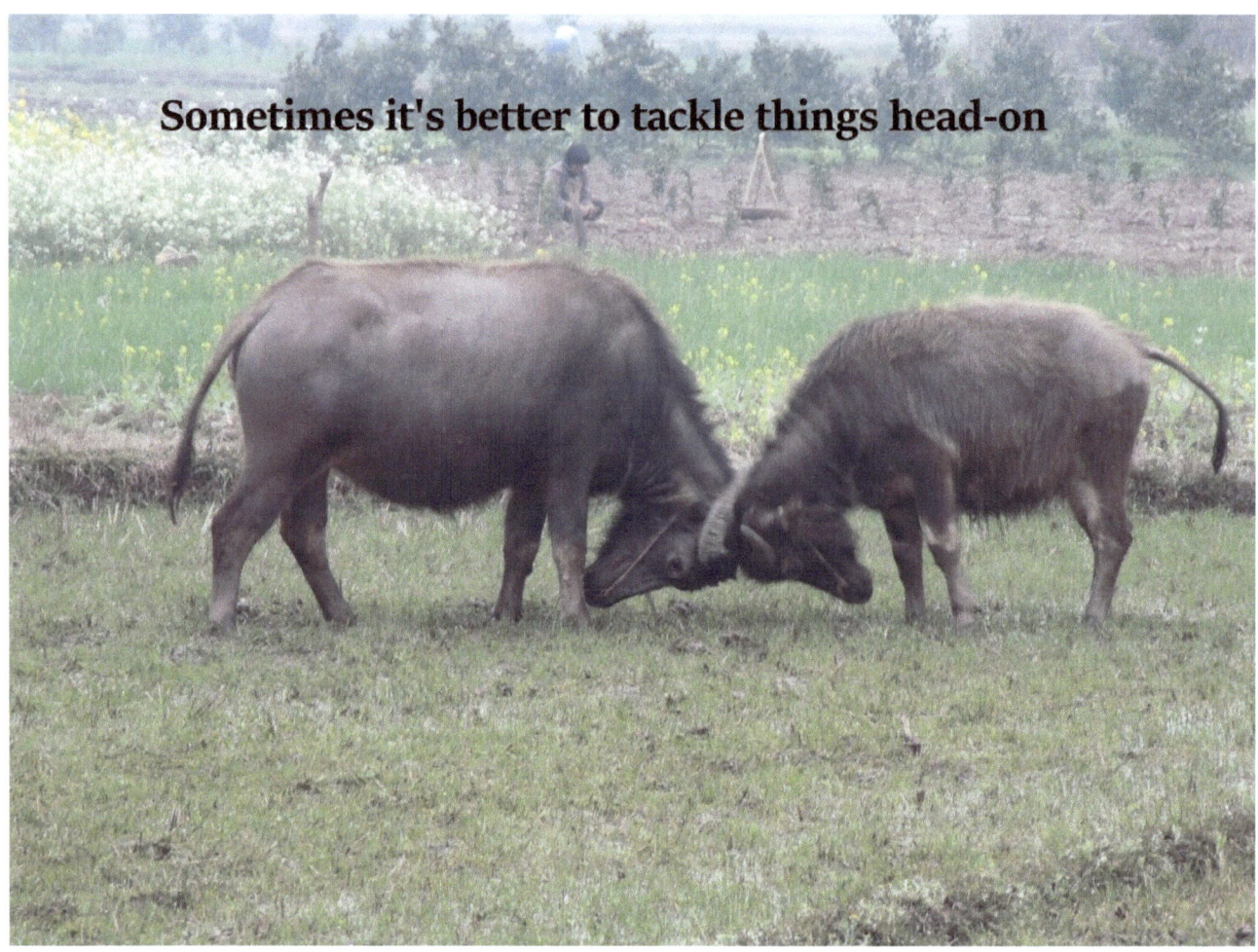

Sometimes it's better to tackle things head-on

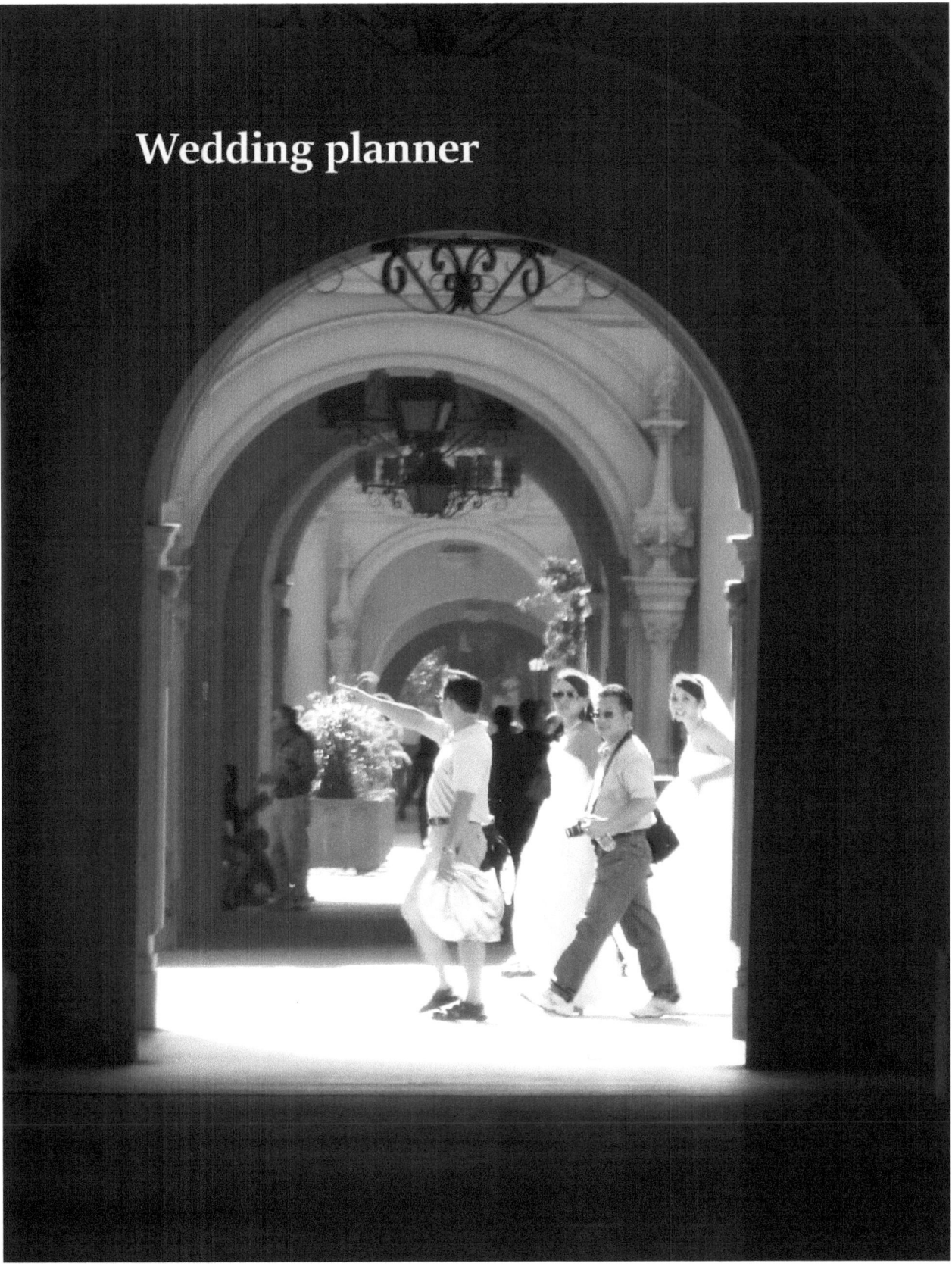

Wedding planner

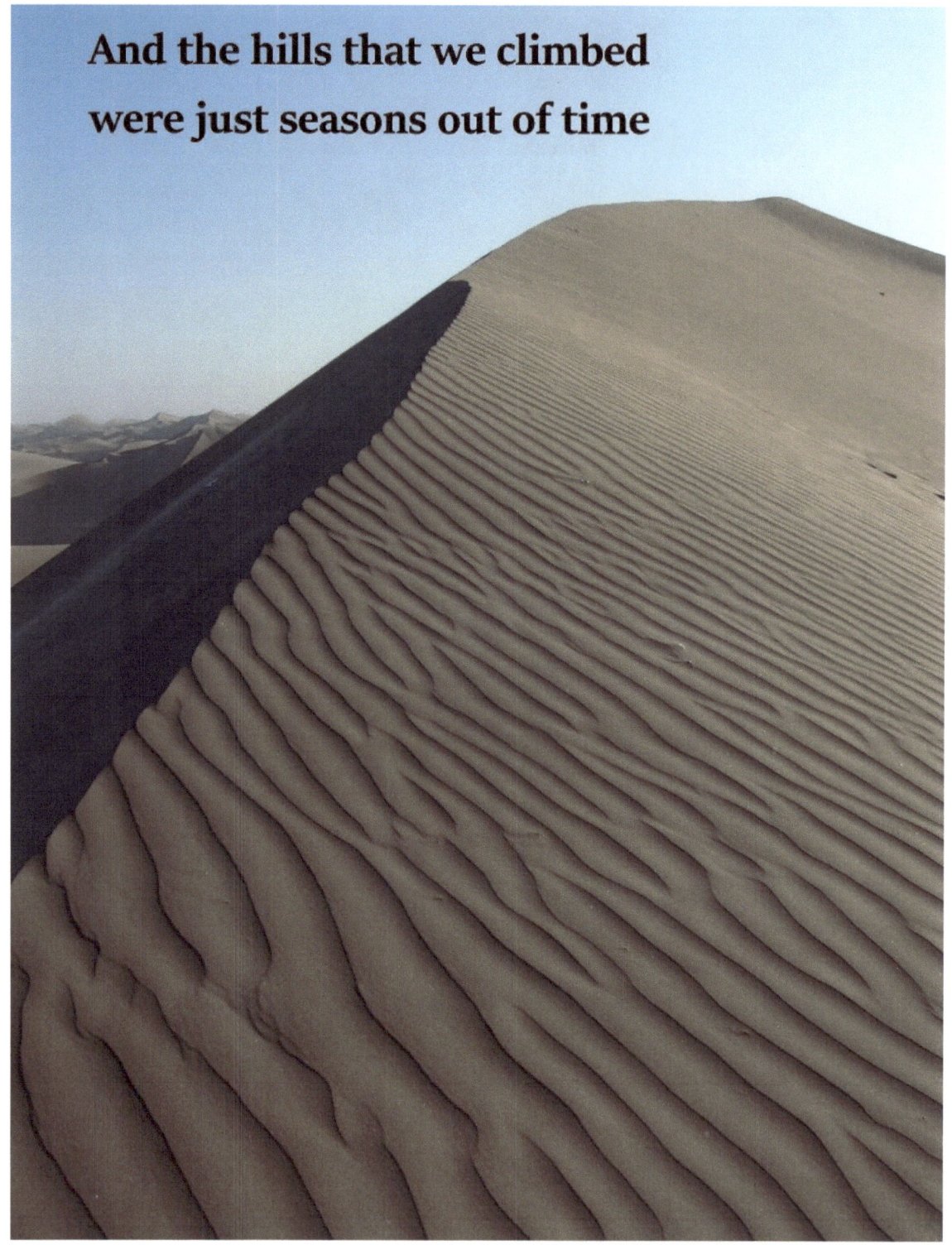

And the hills that we climbed

were just seasons out of time

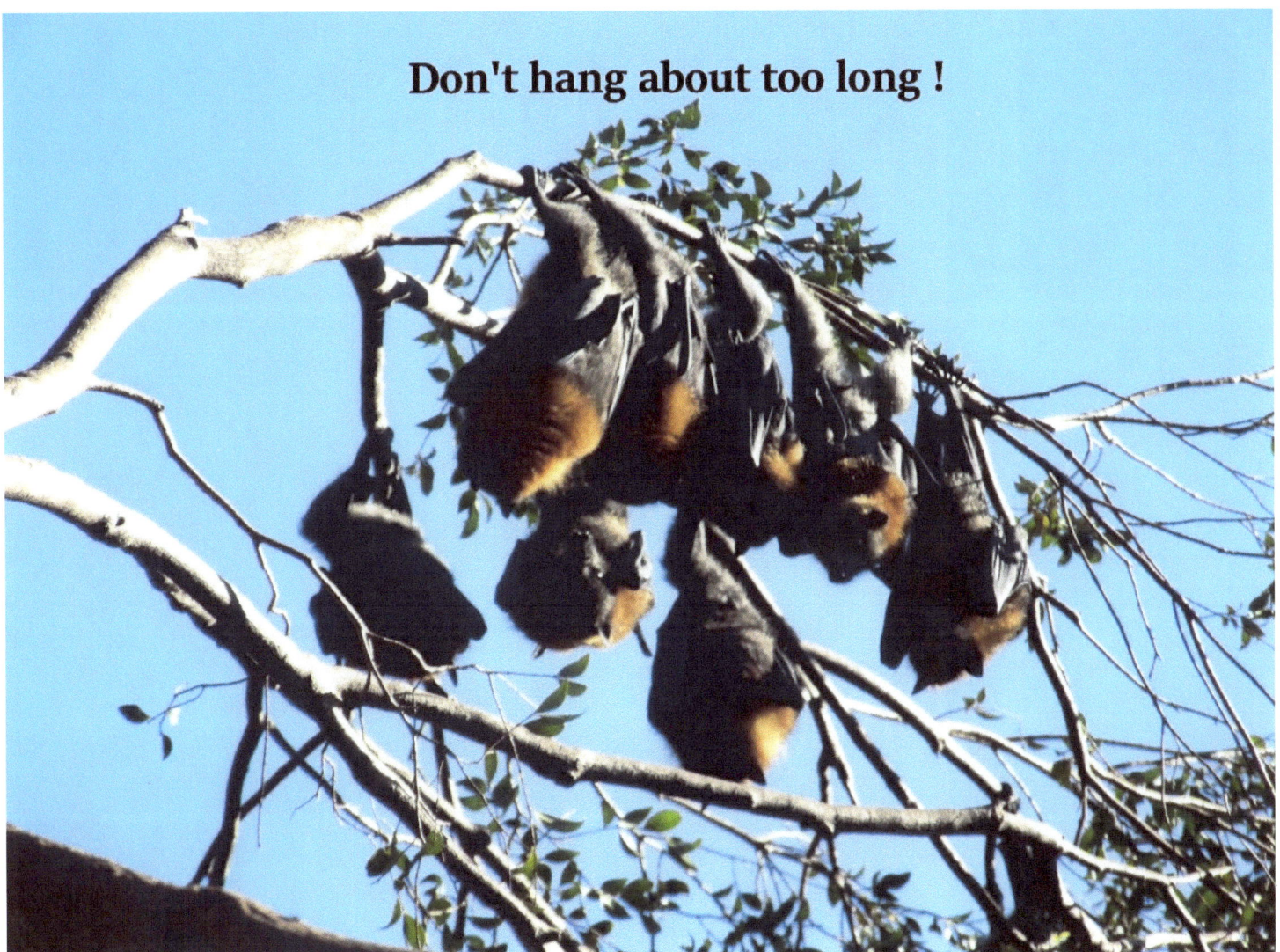

Don't hang about too long !

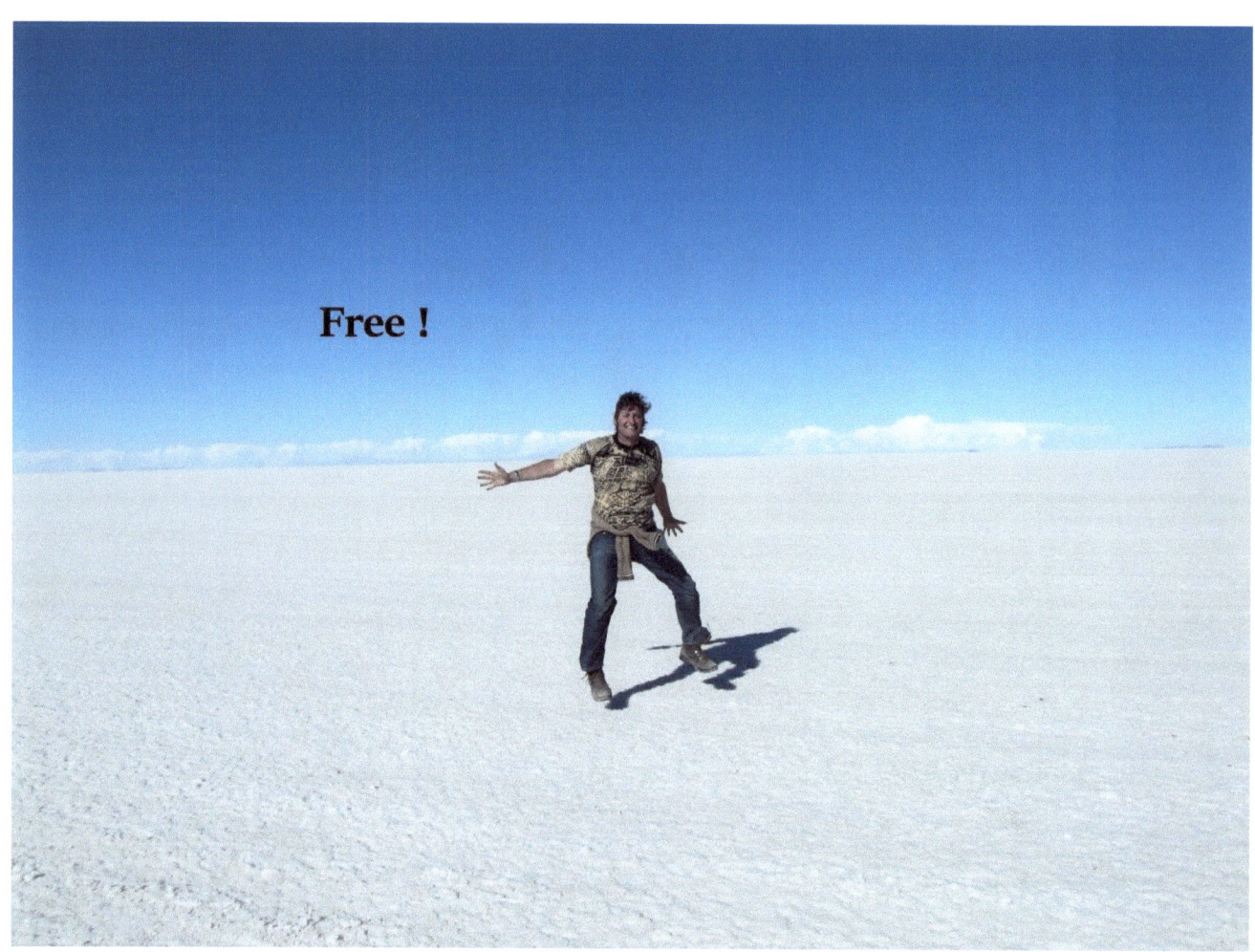

Free !

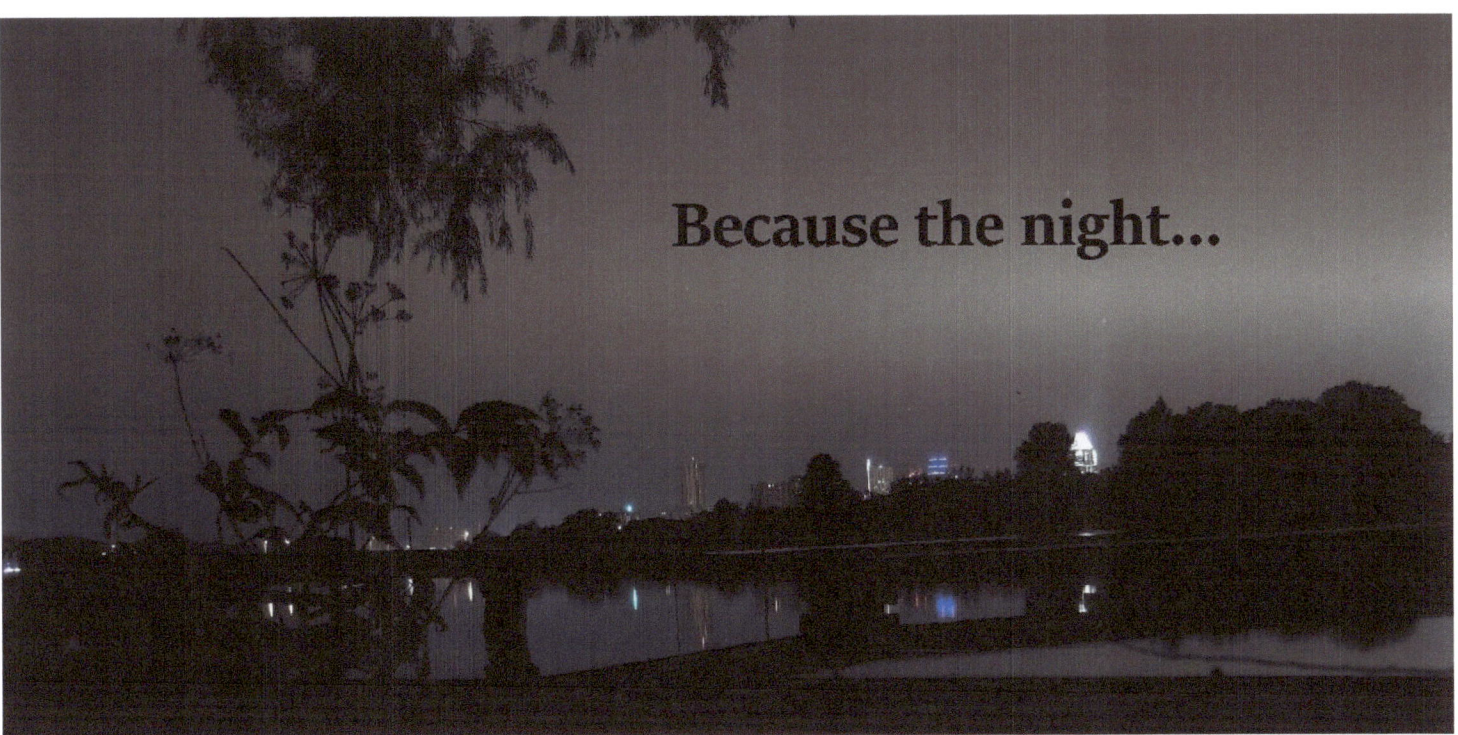

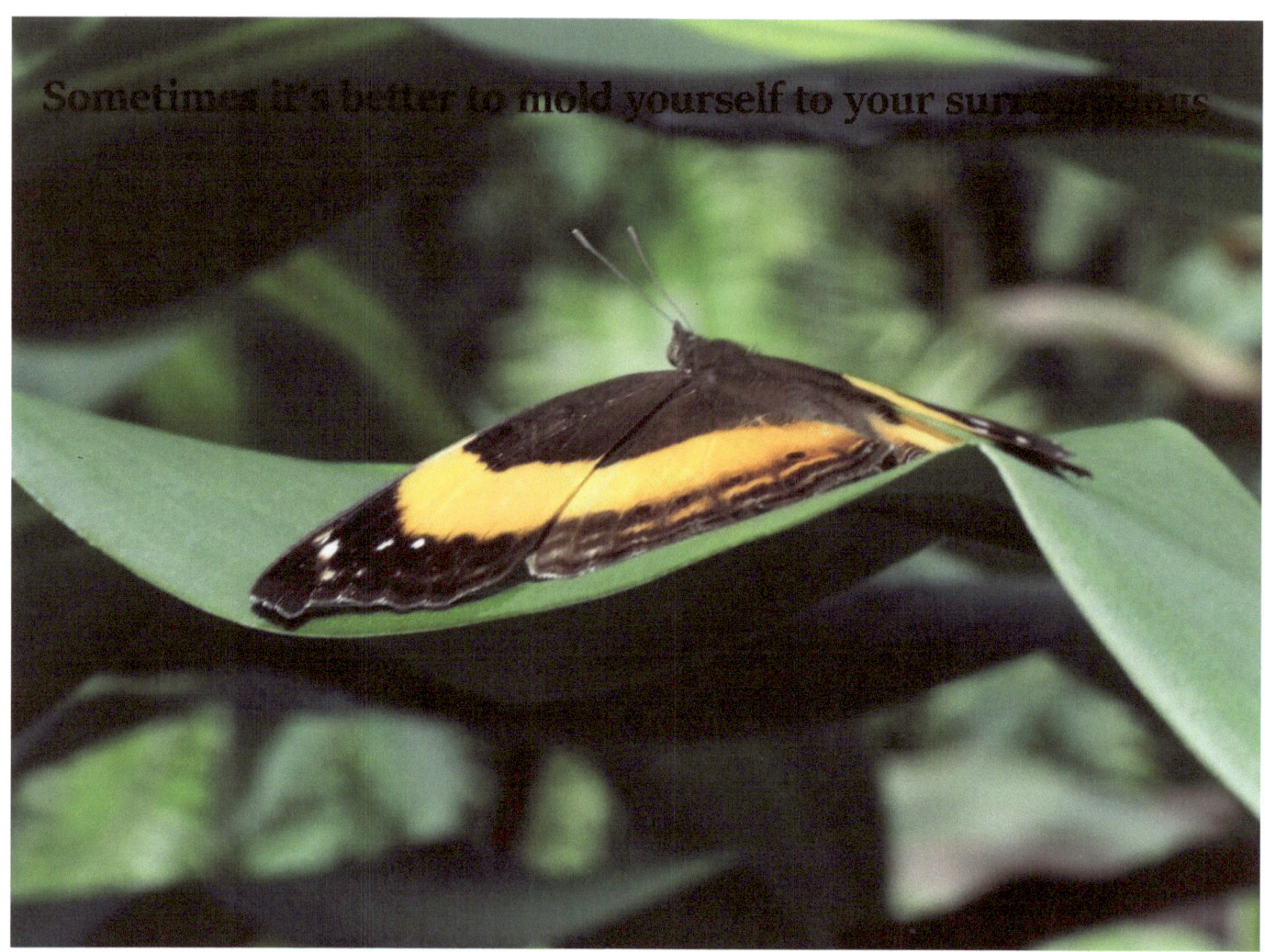

Sometimes it's better to mold yourself to your surroundings

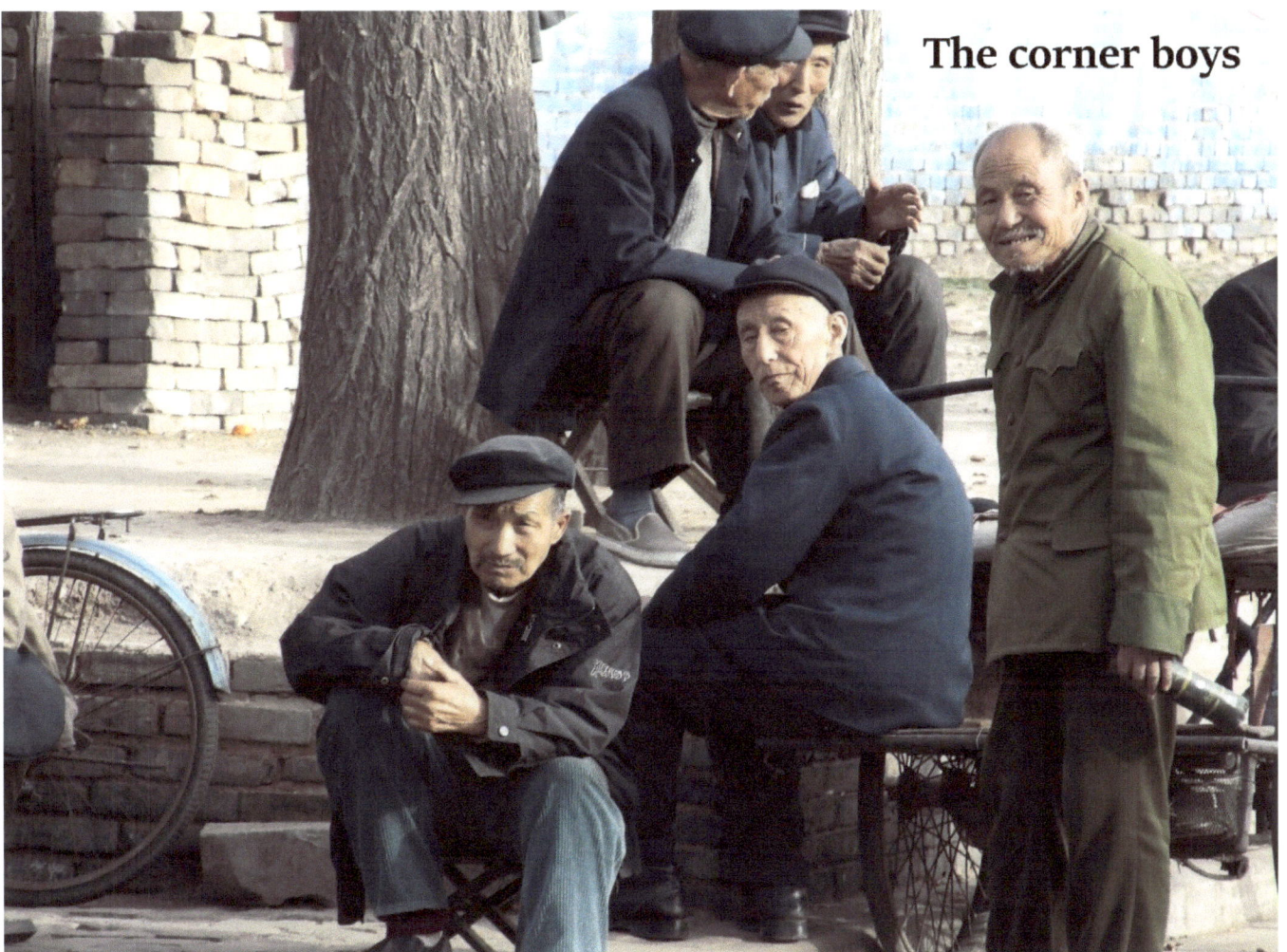

The corner boys

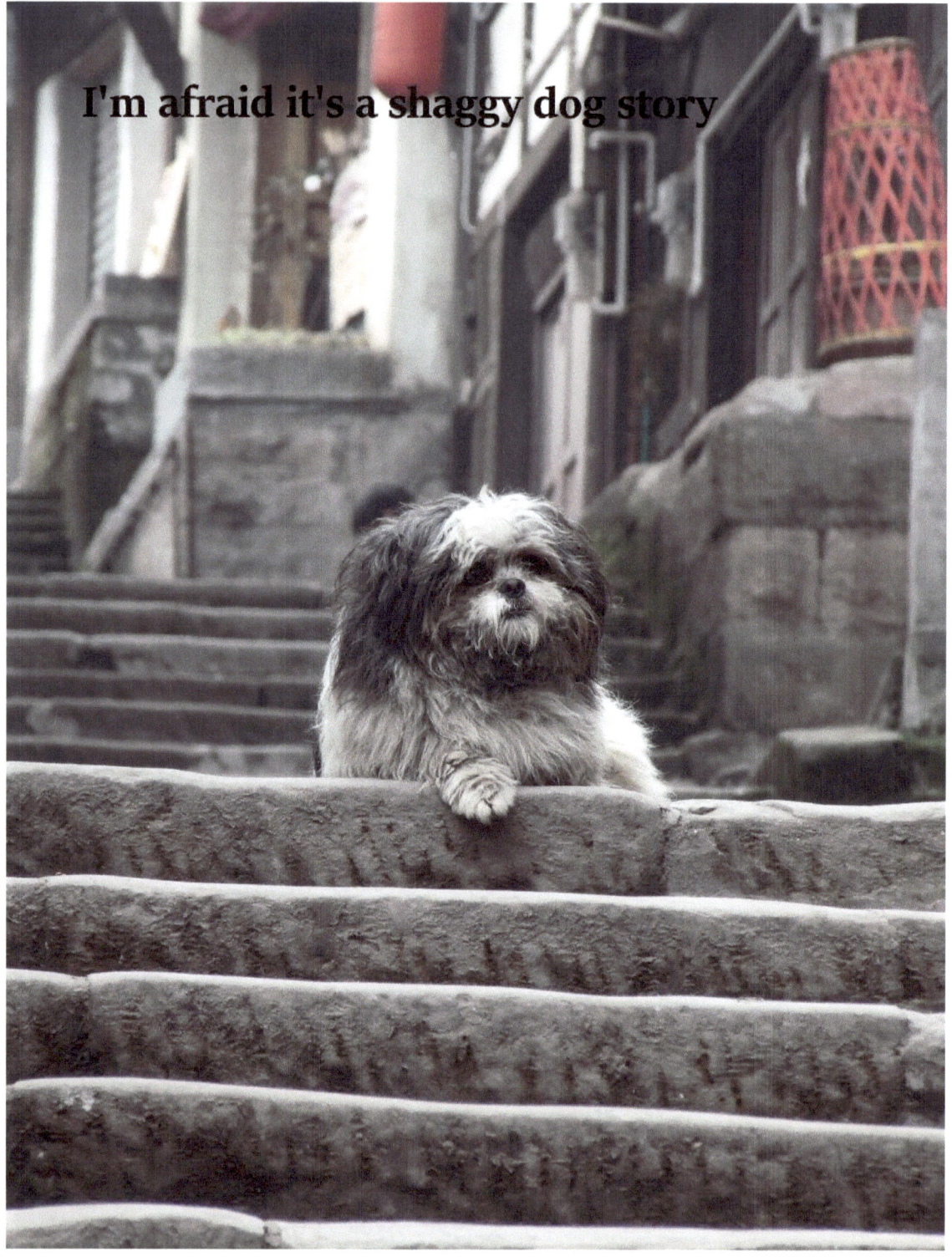

I'm afraid it's a shaggy dog story

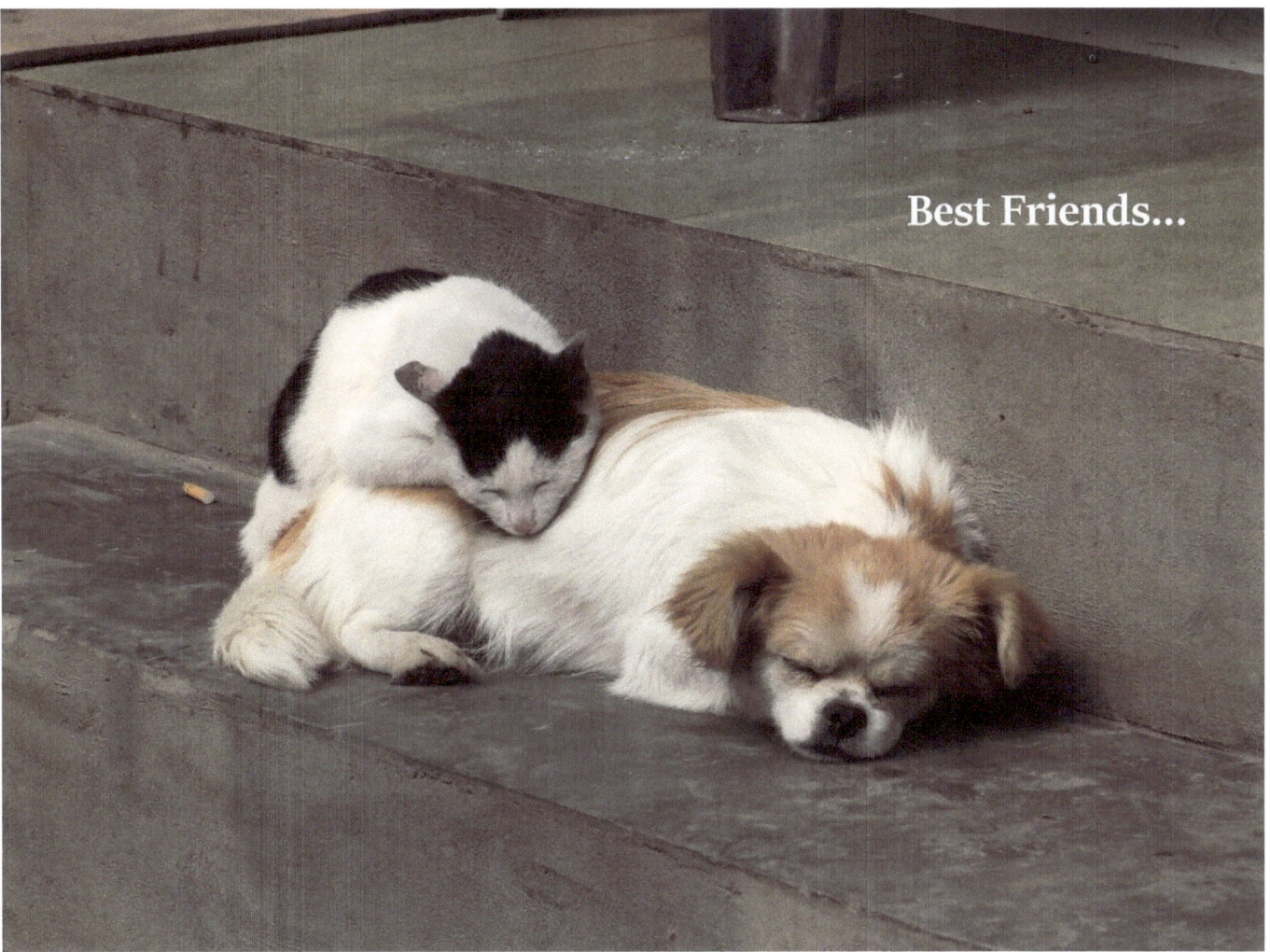

Best Friends...

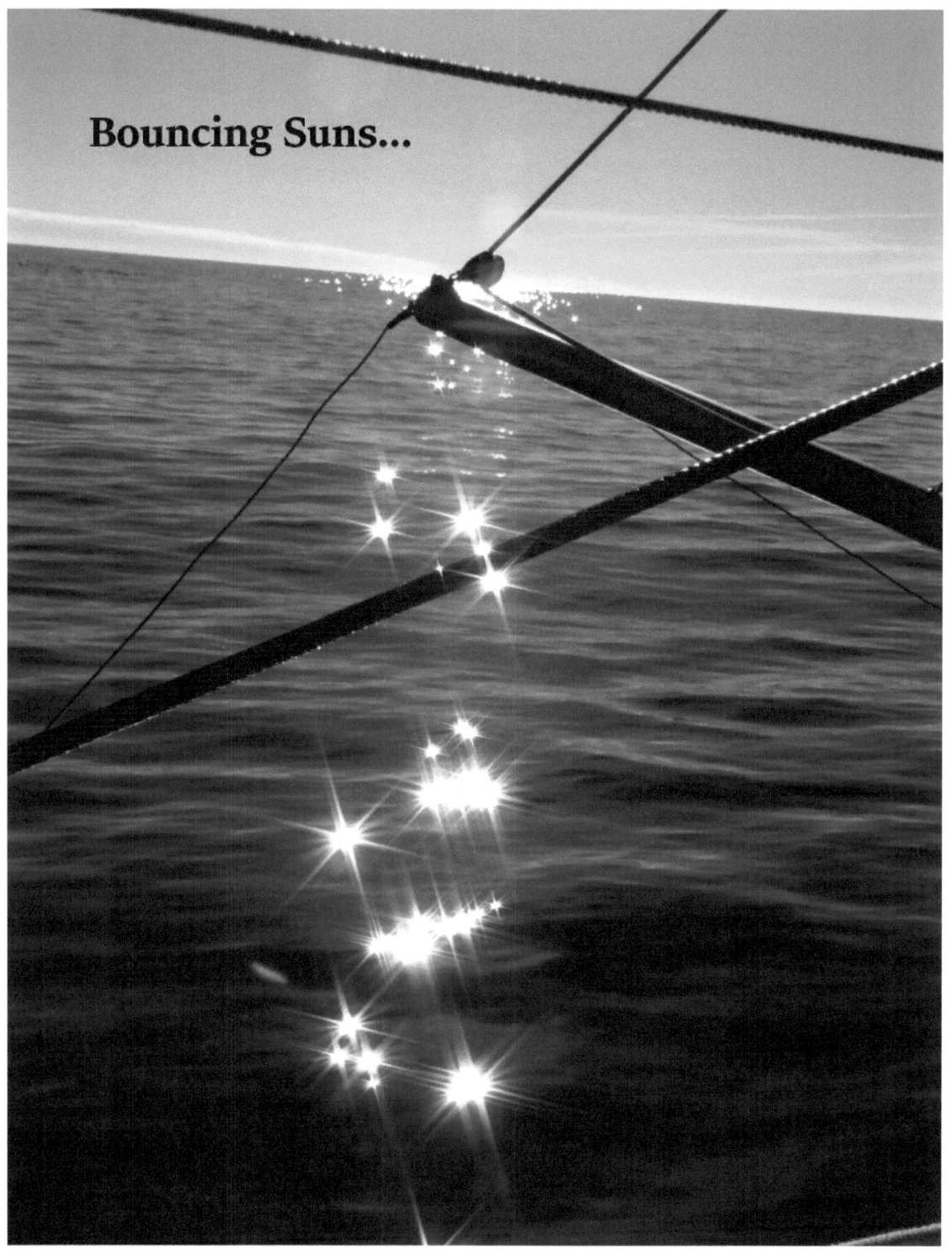

Enjoy the moment !

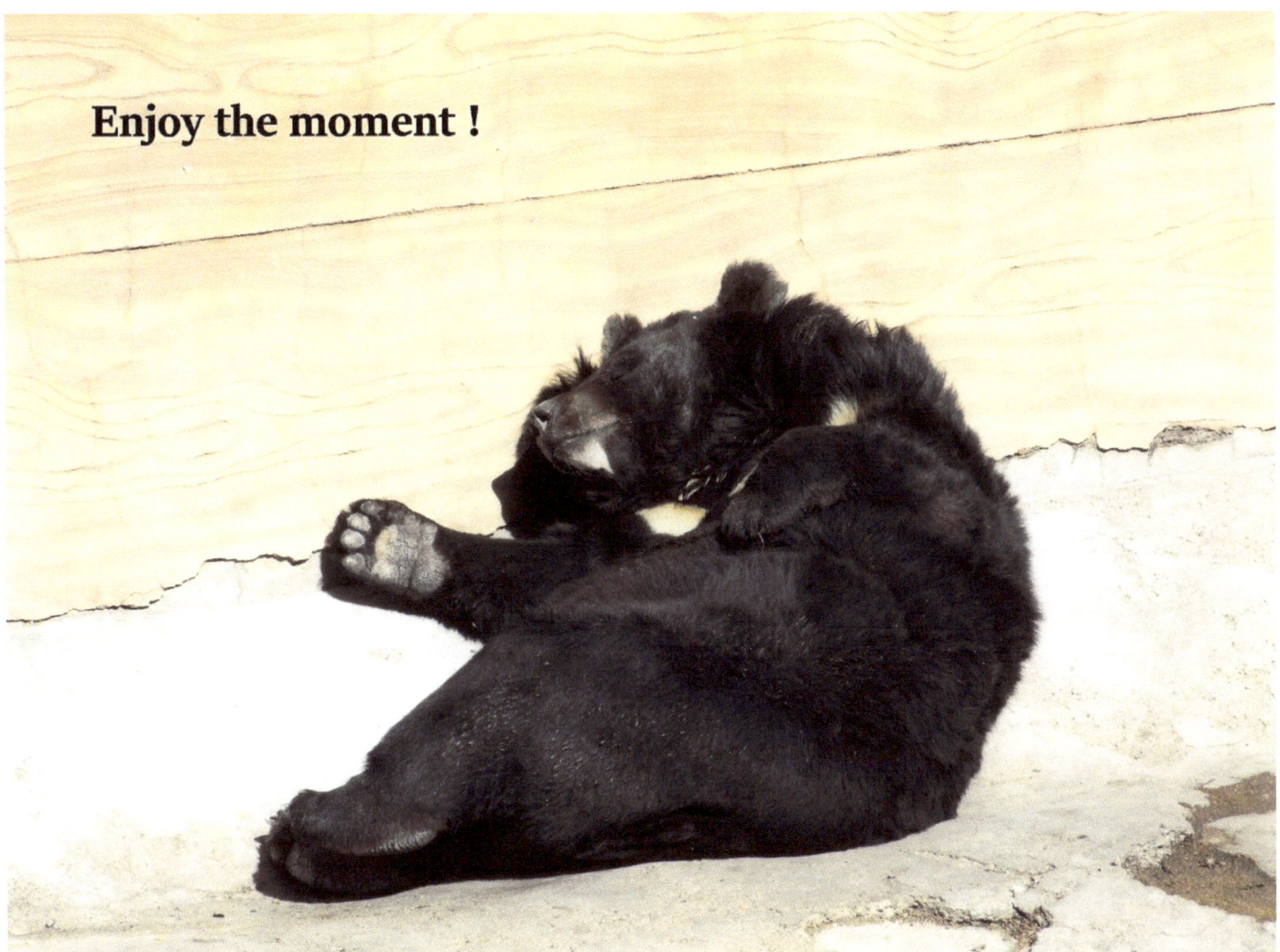

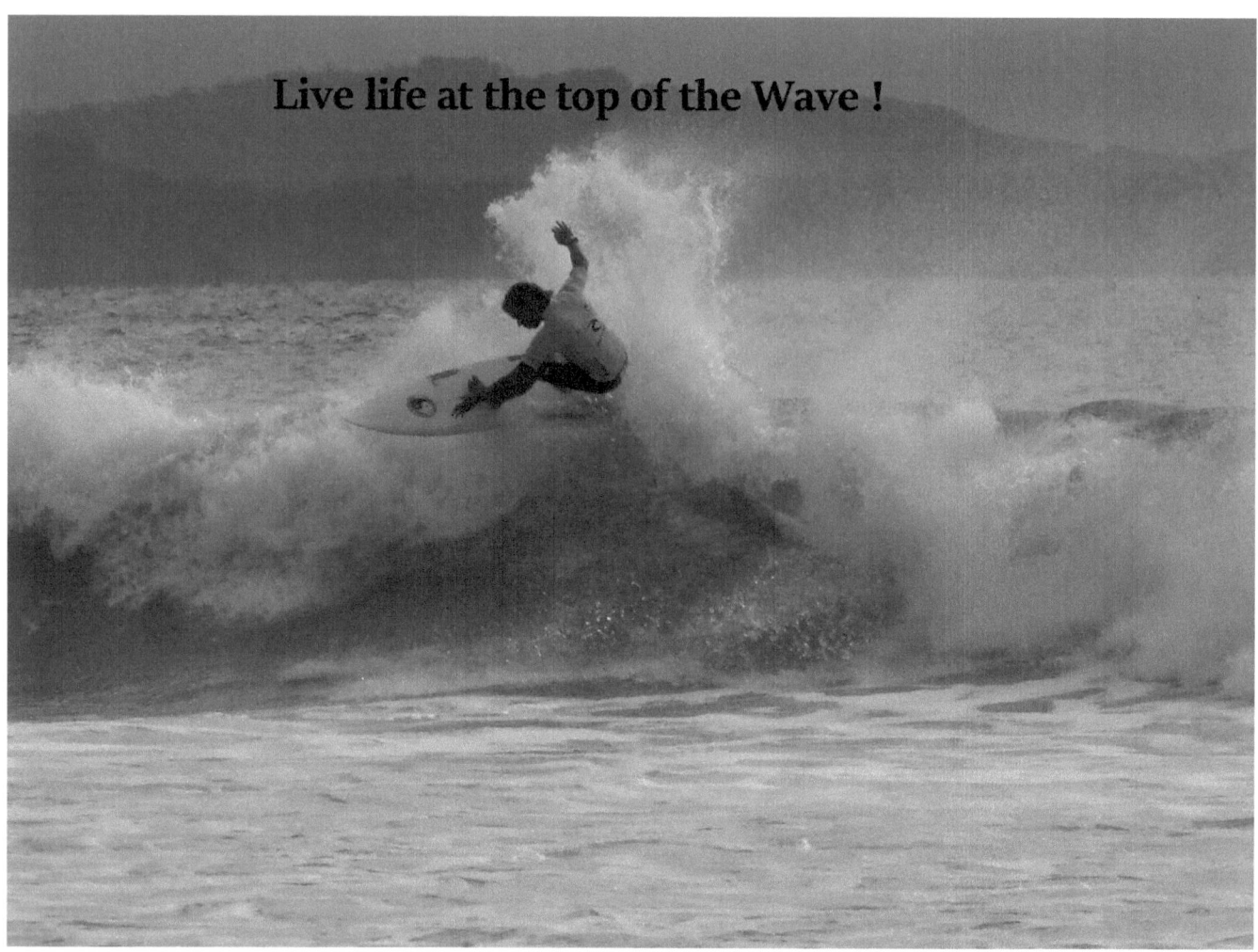

Live life at the top of the Wave !

Don't wake me up
too early

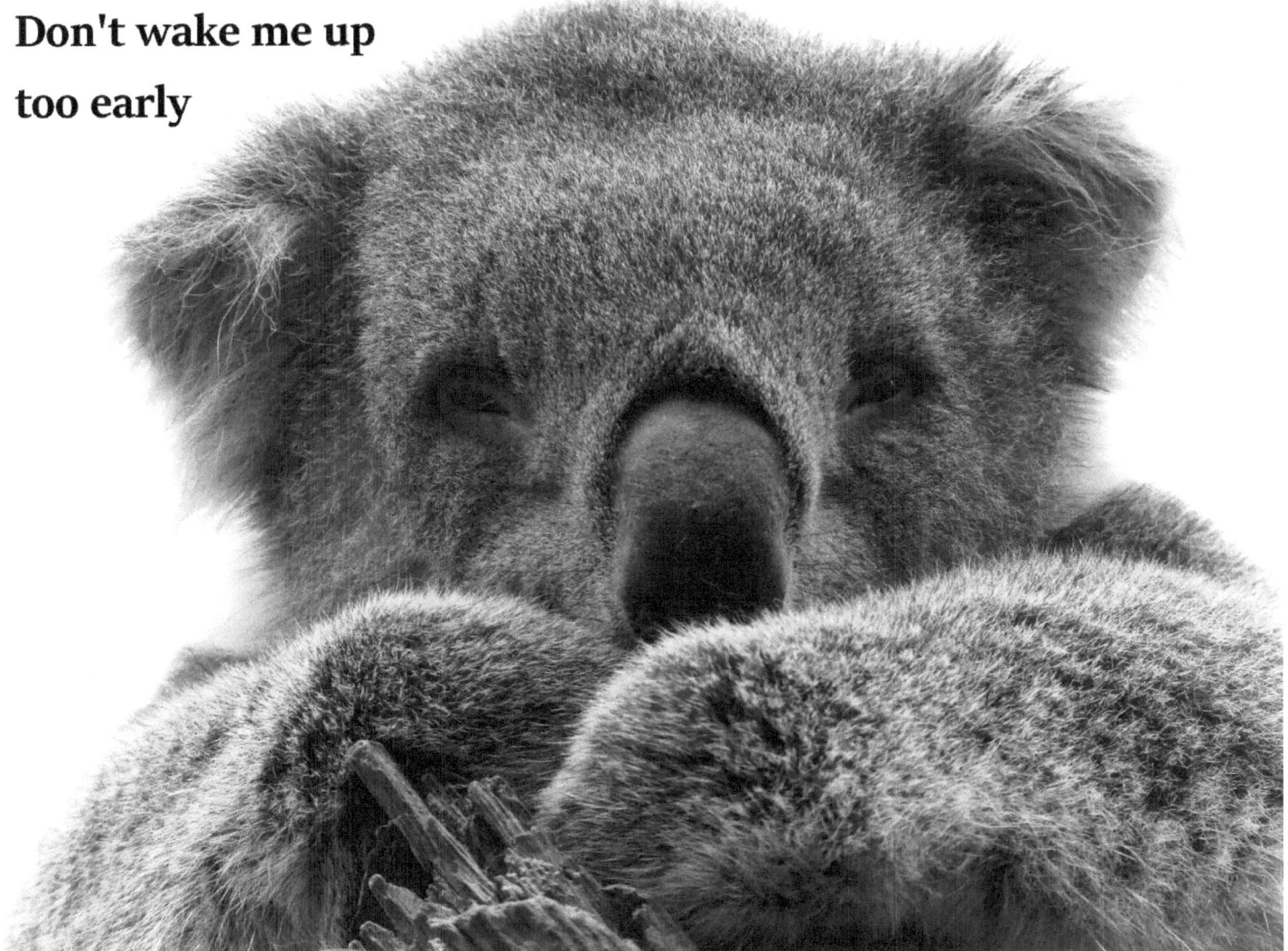

N/A

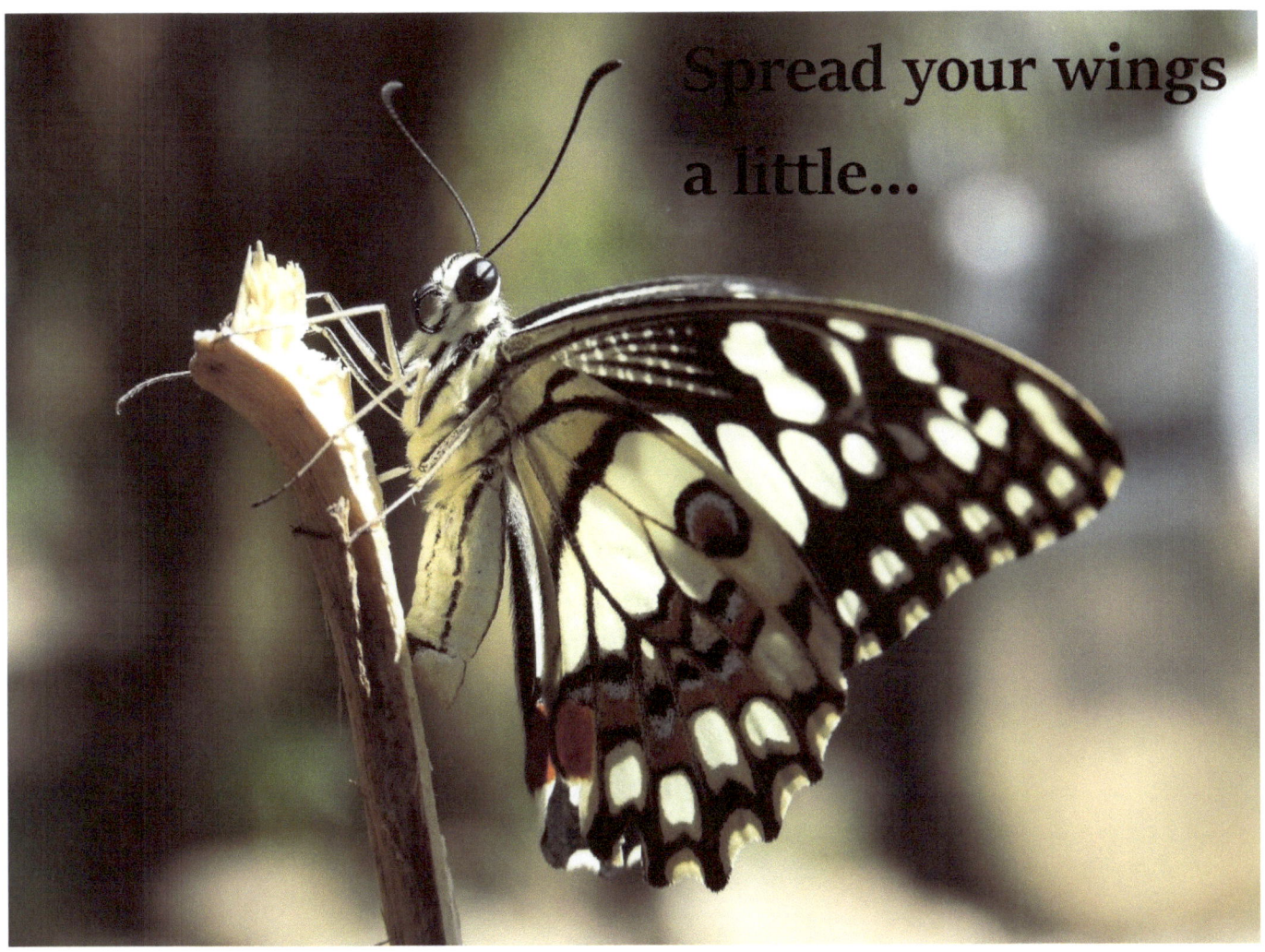

Spread your wings
a little...

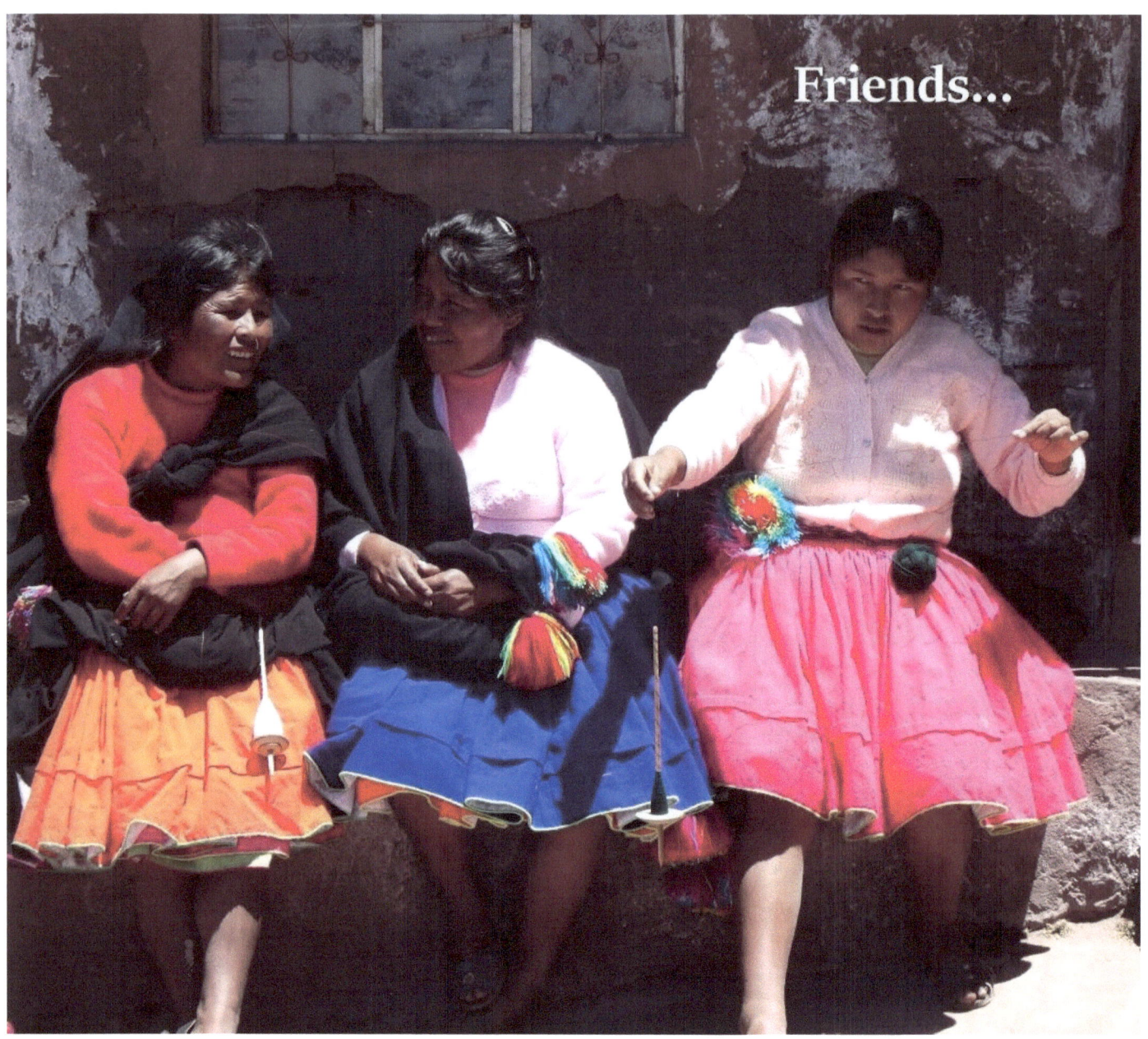

Friends...

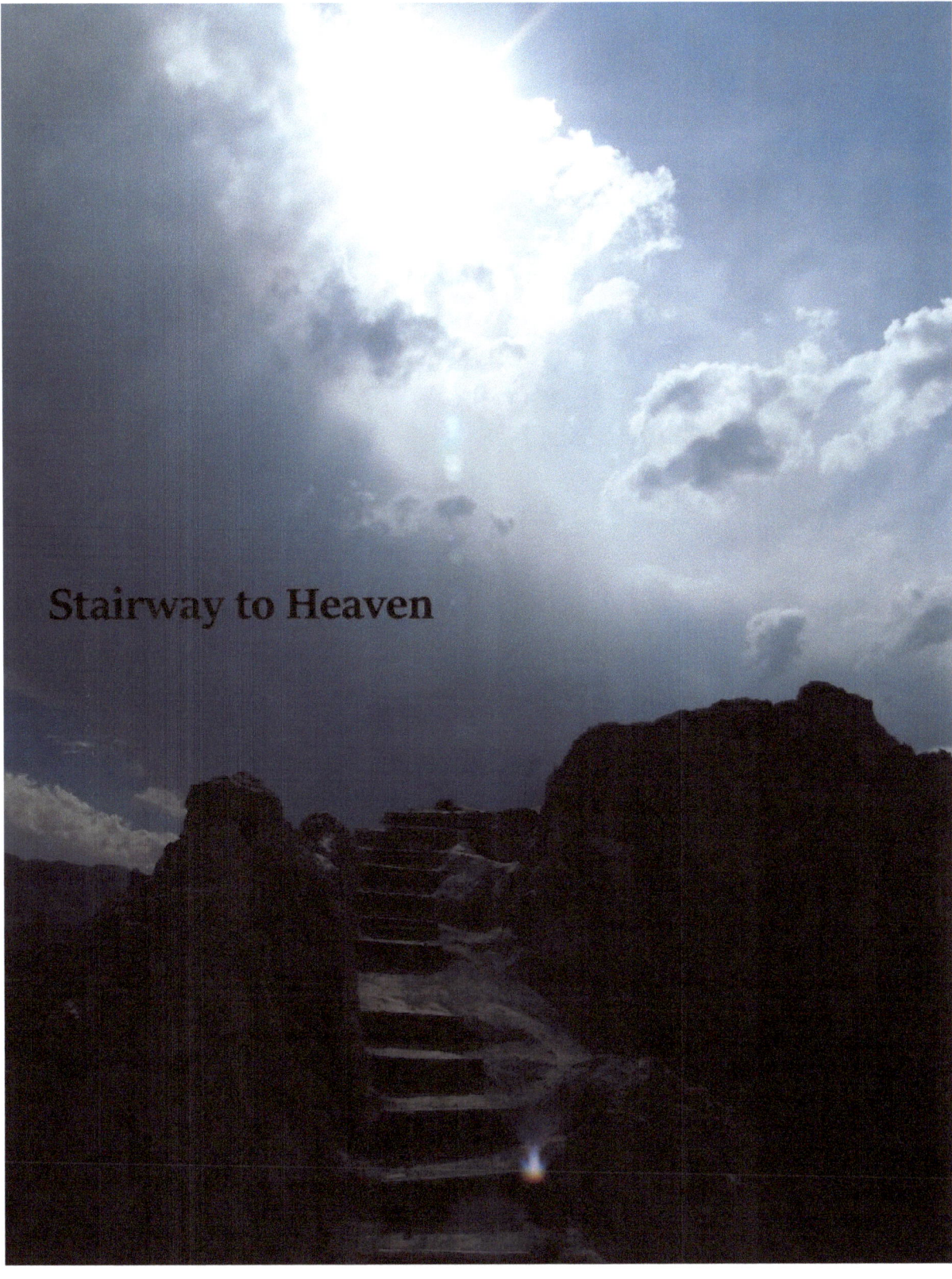

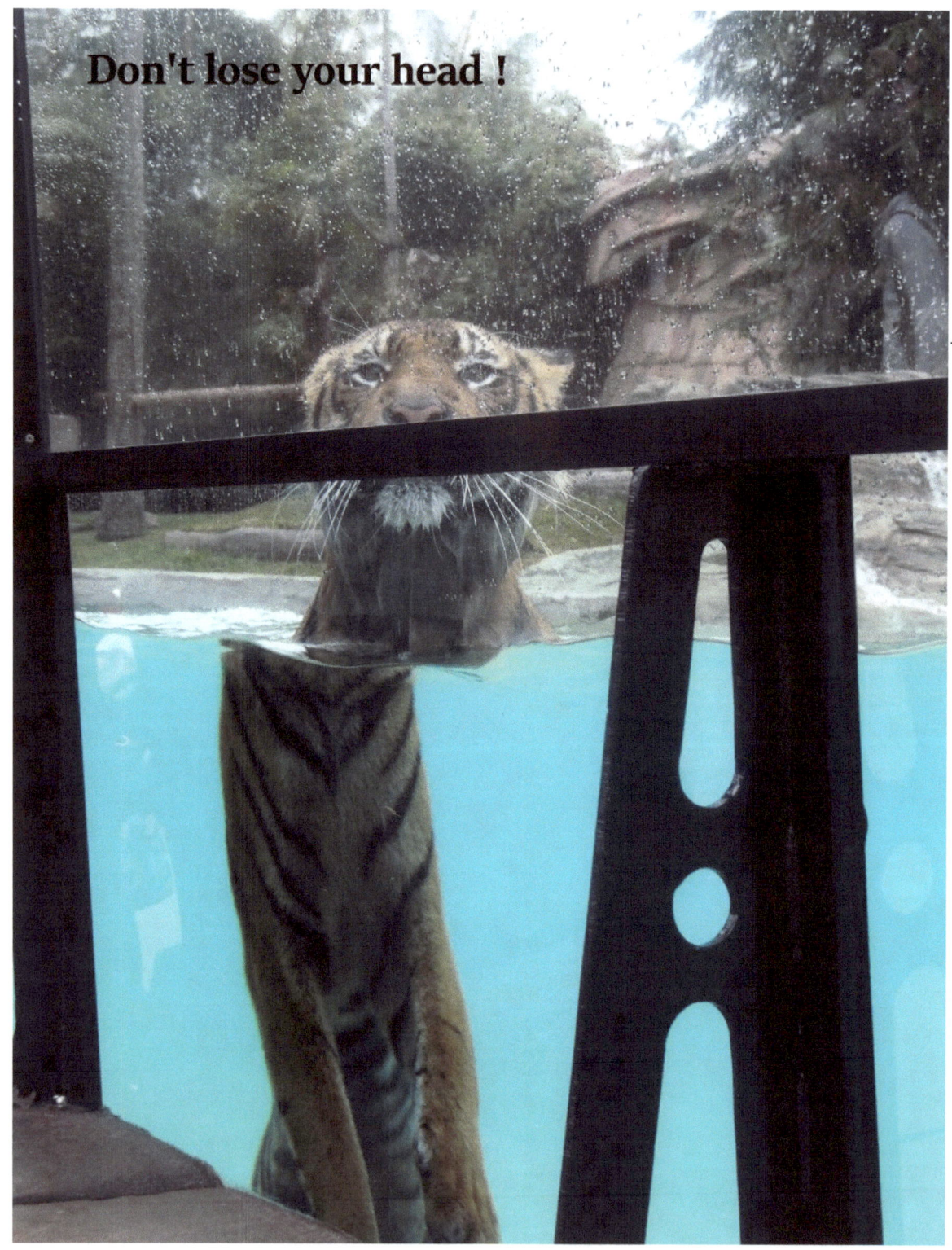

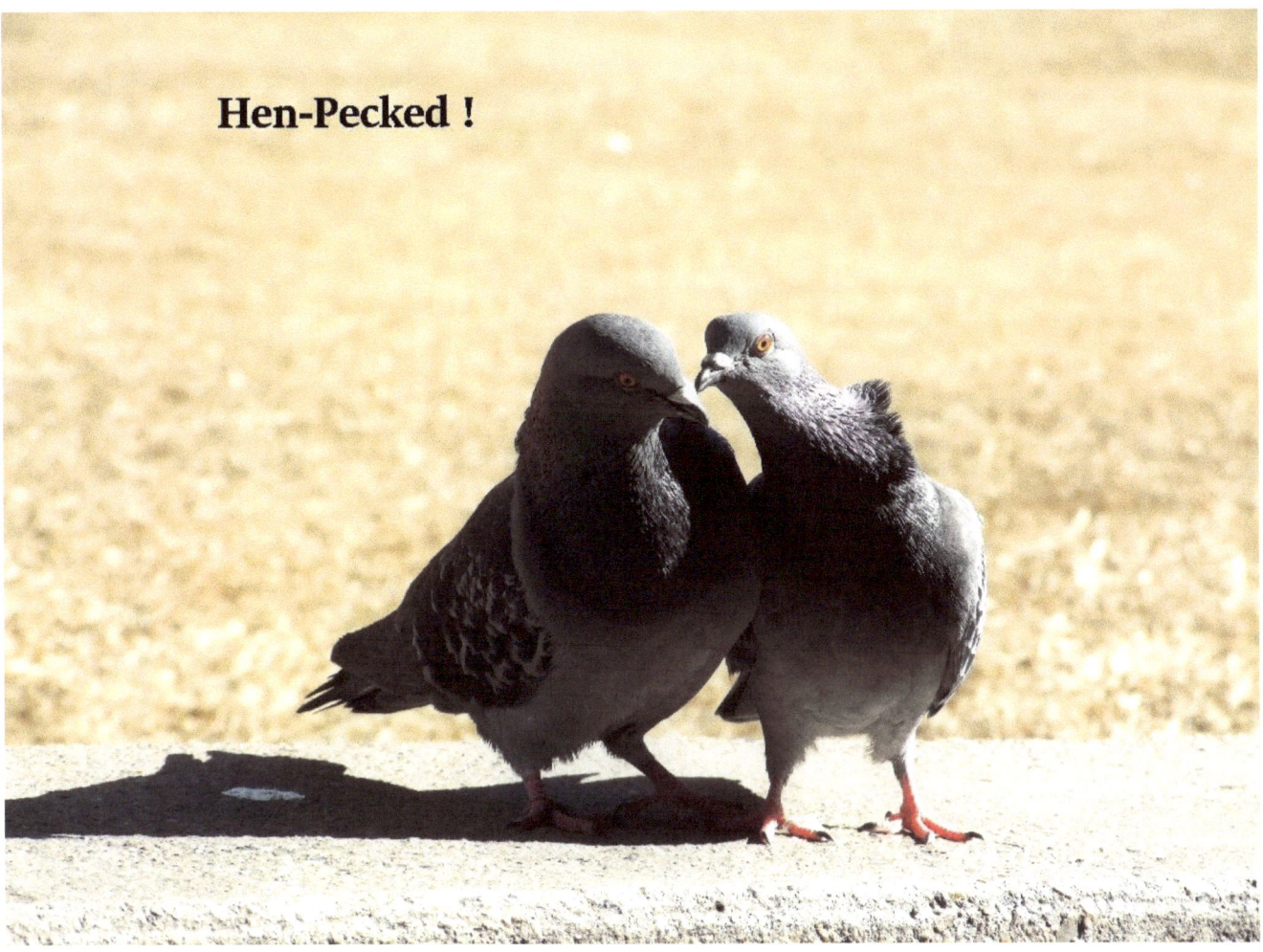

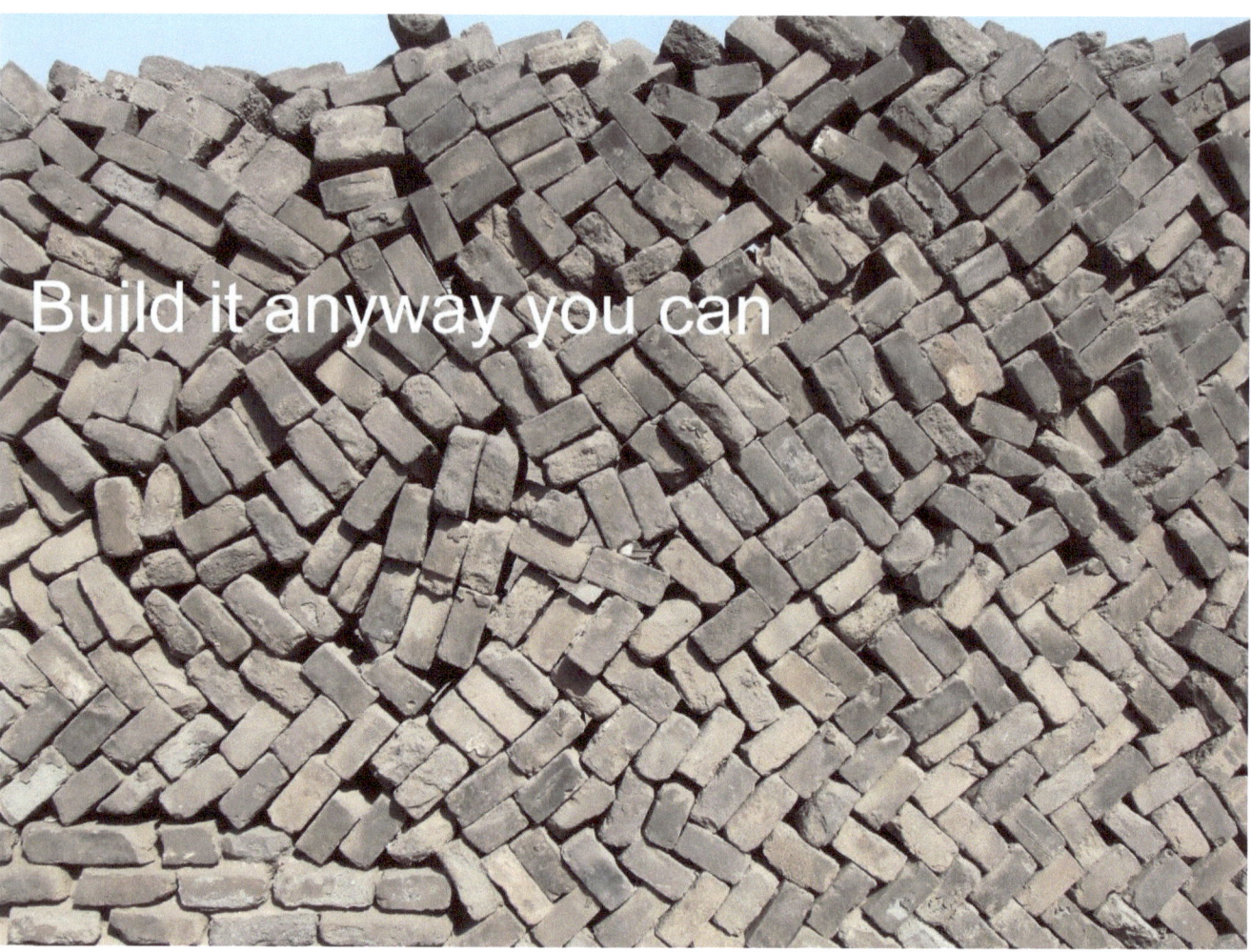

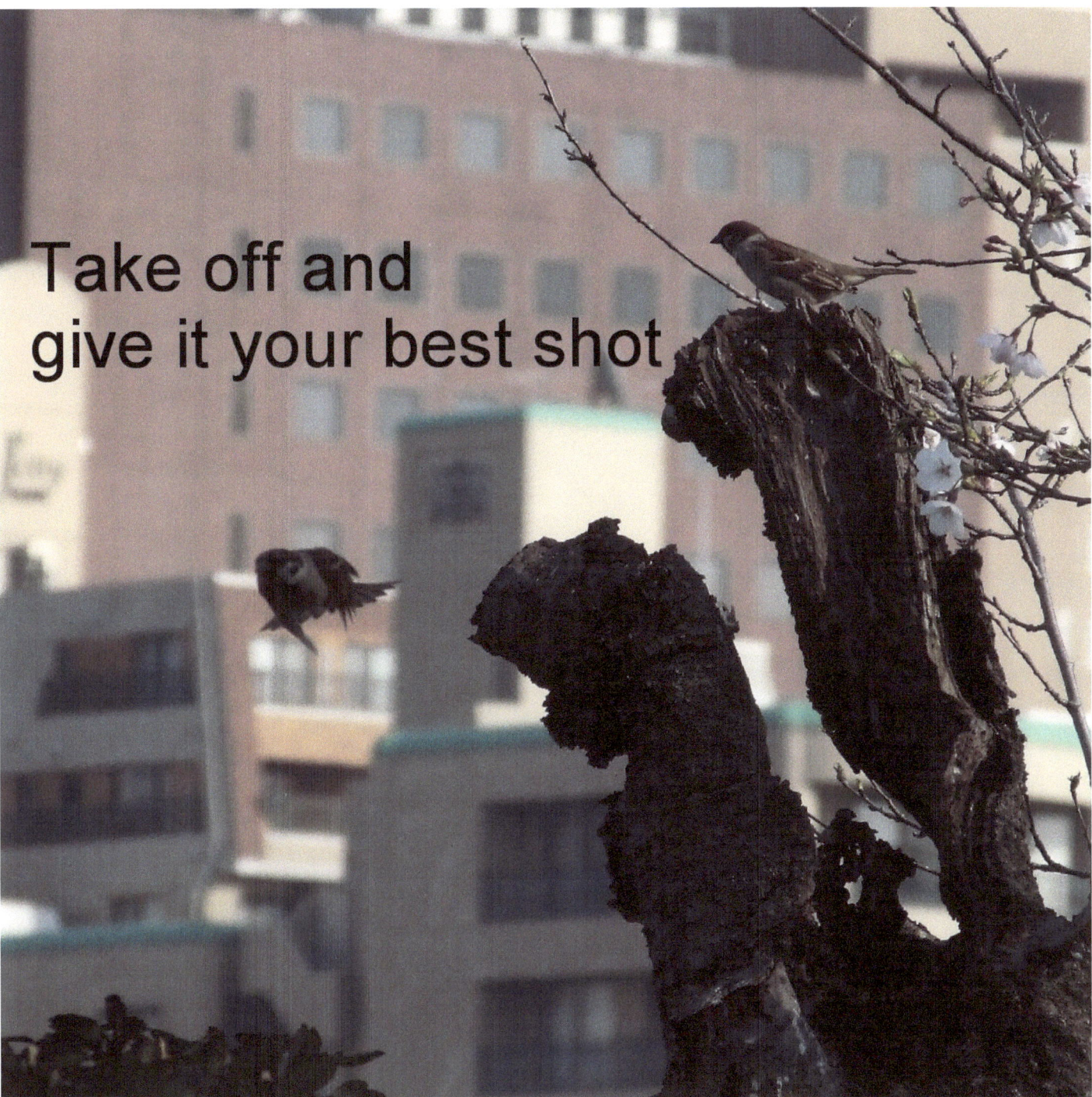

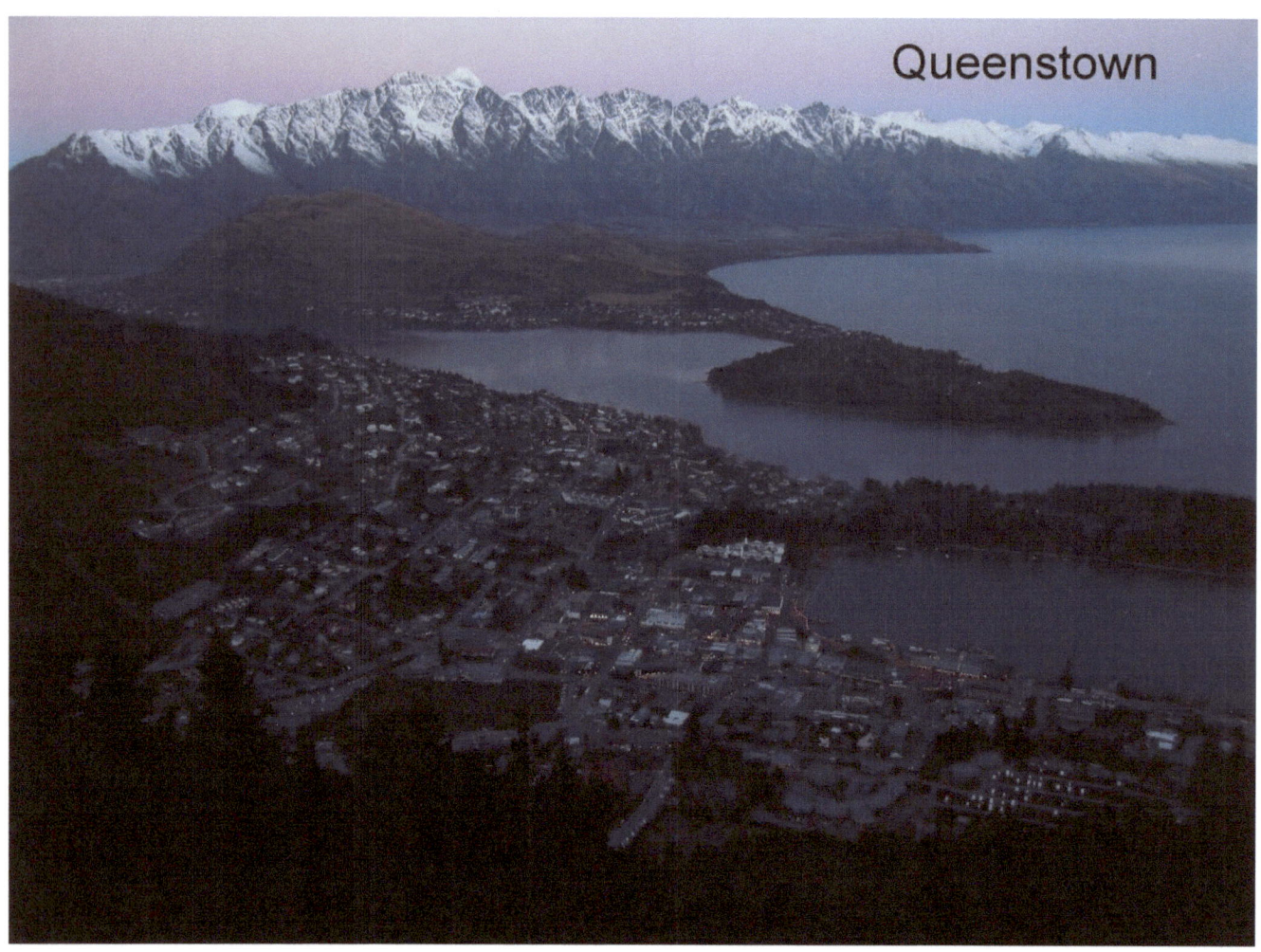

Queenstown

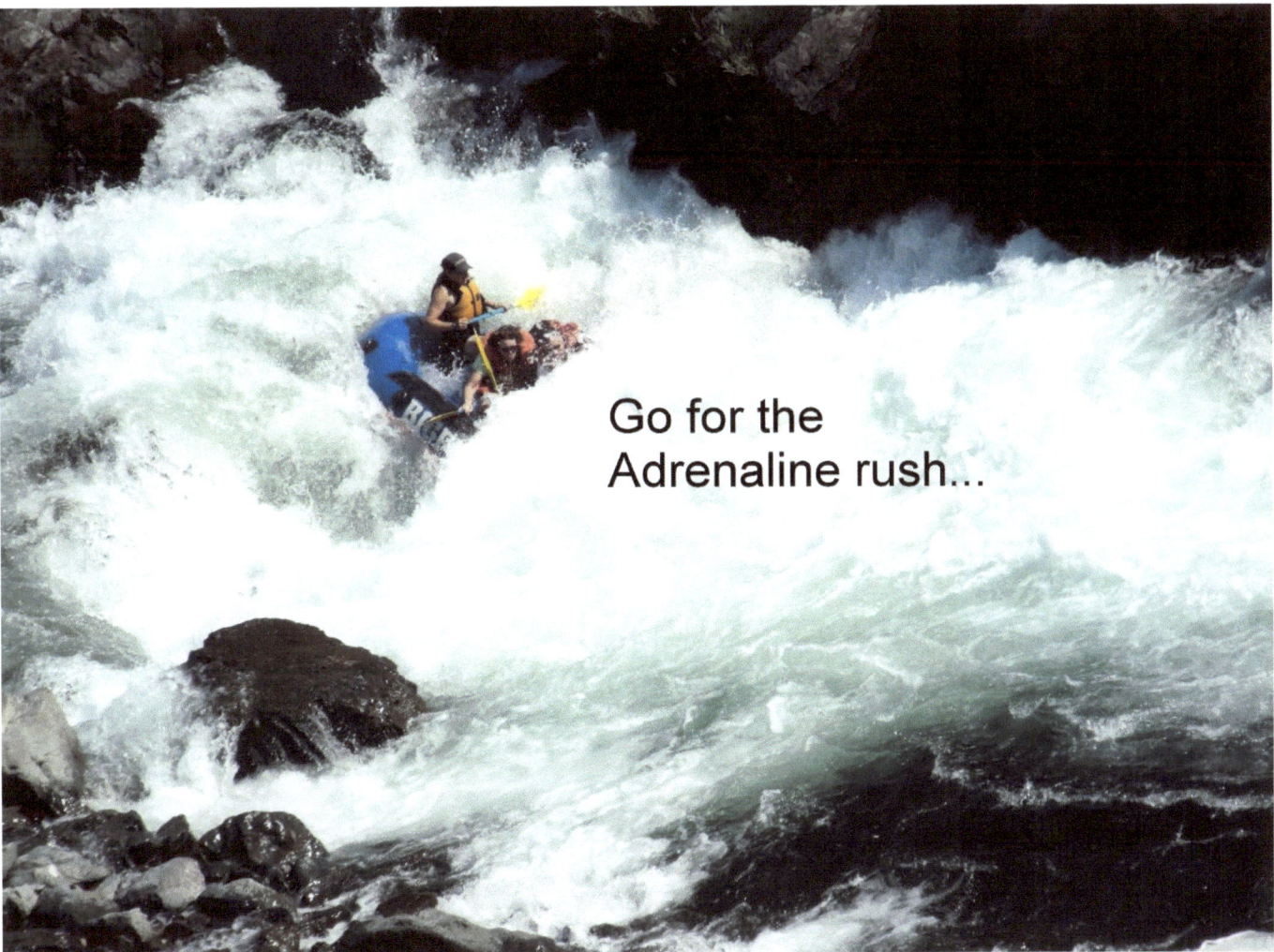

Go for the
Adrenaline rush...

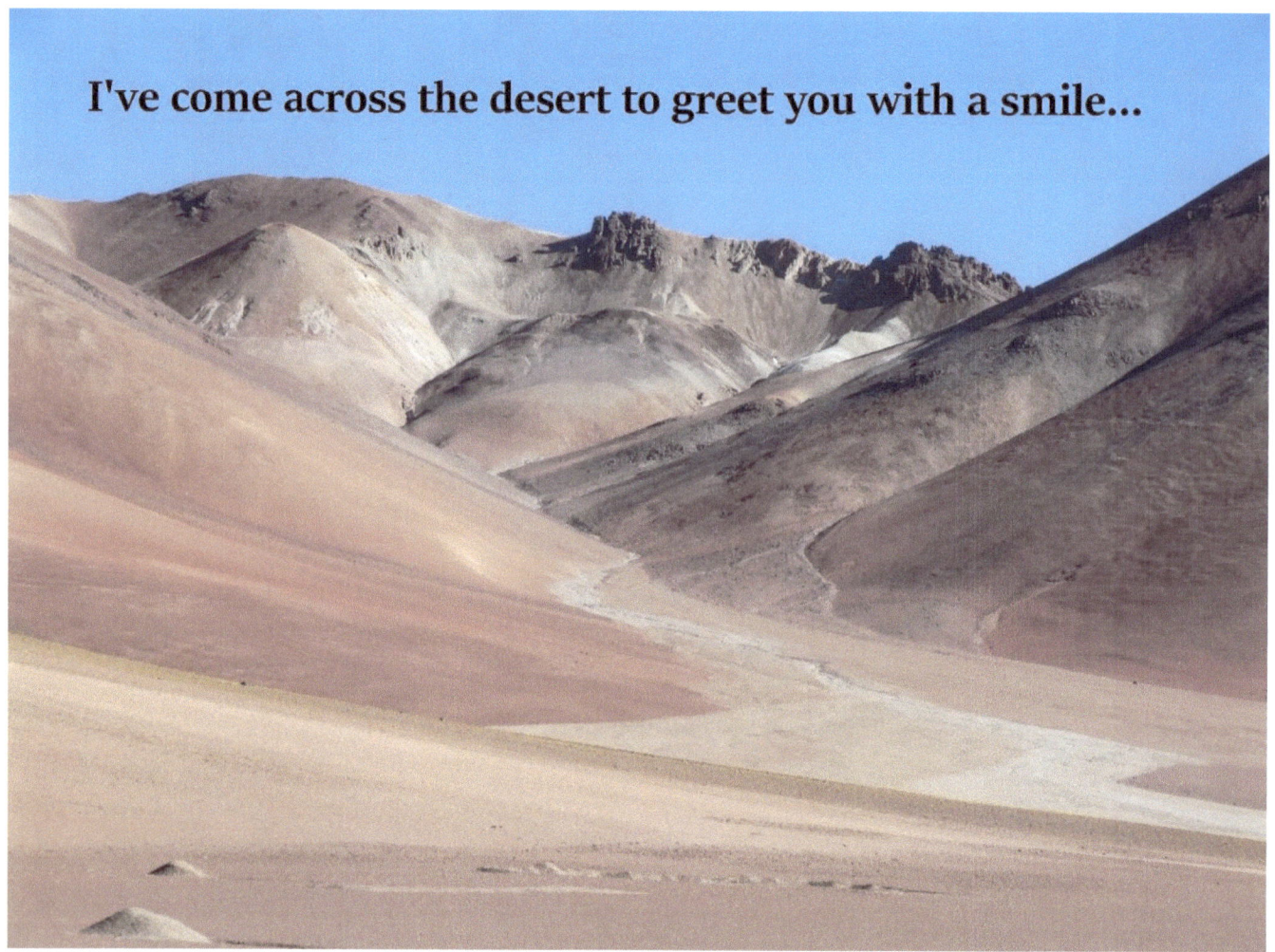

I've come across the desert to greet you with a smile...

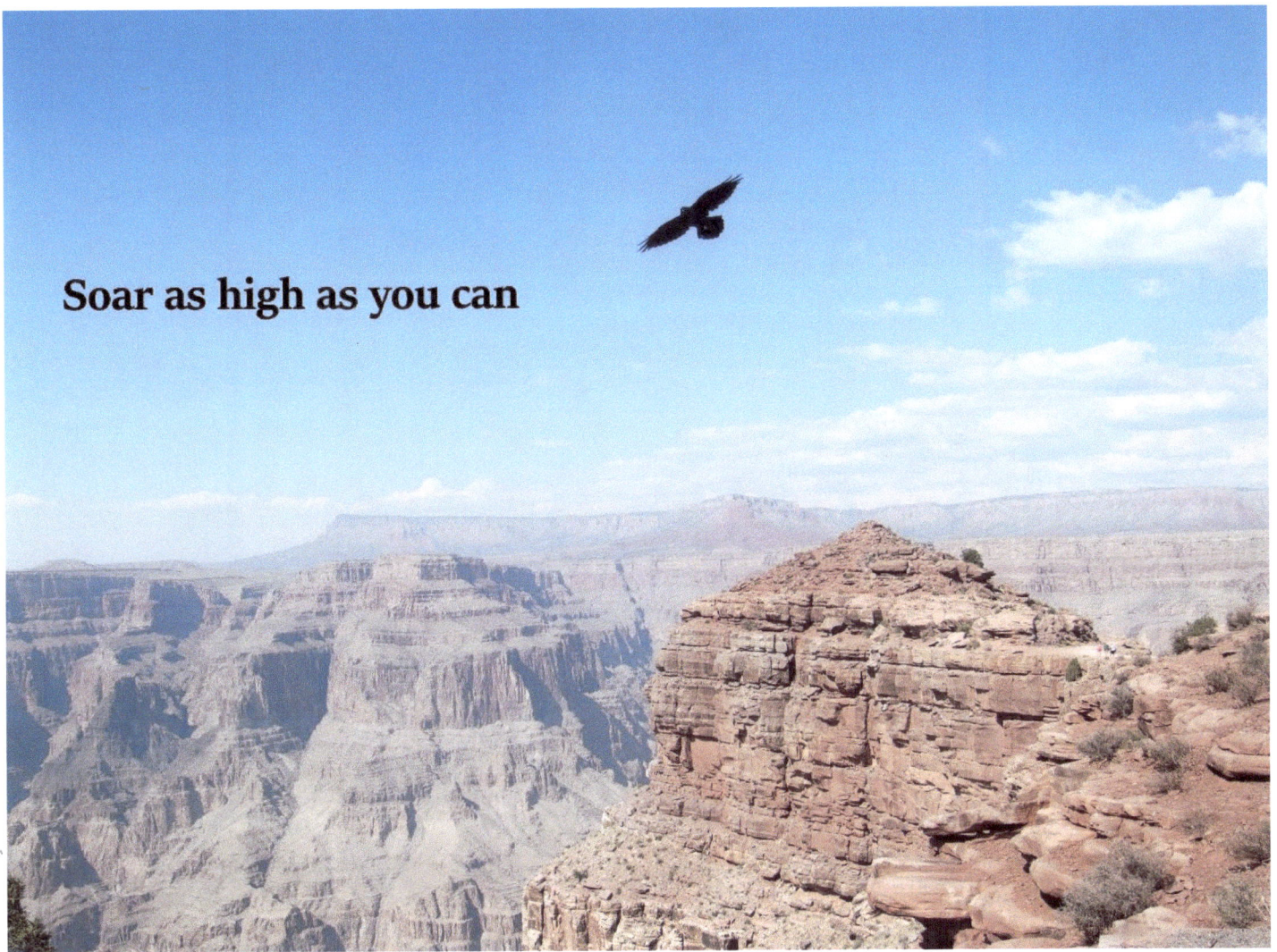

Soar as high as you can

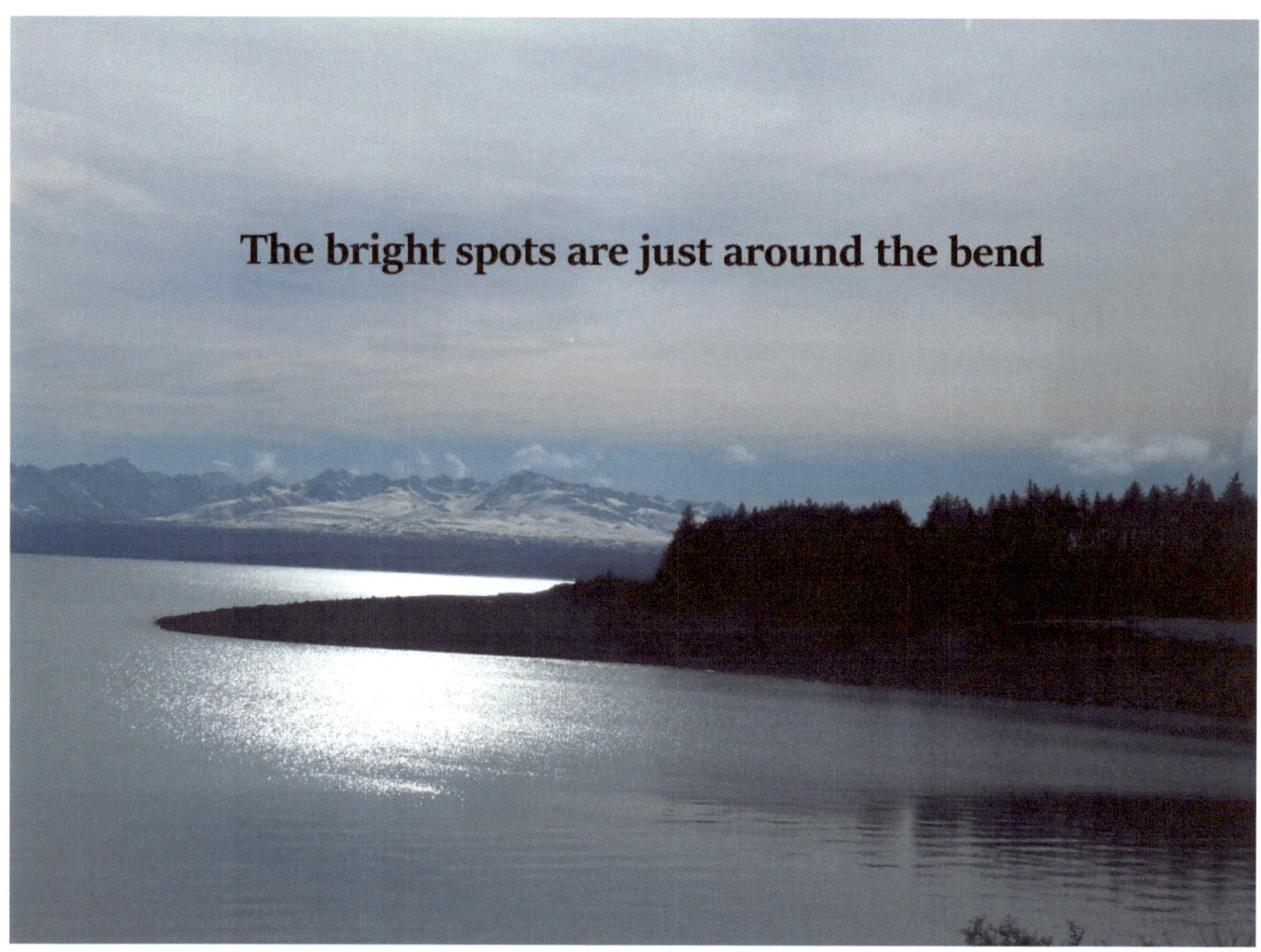

The bright spots are just around the bend

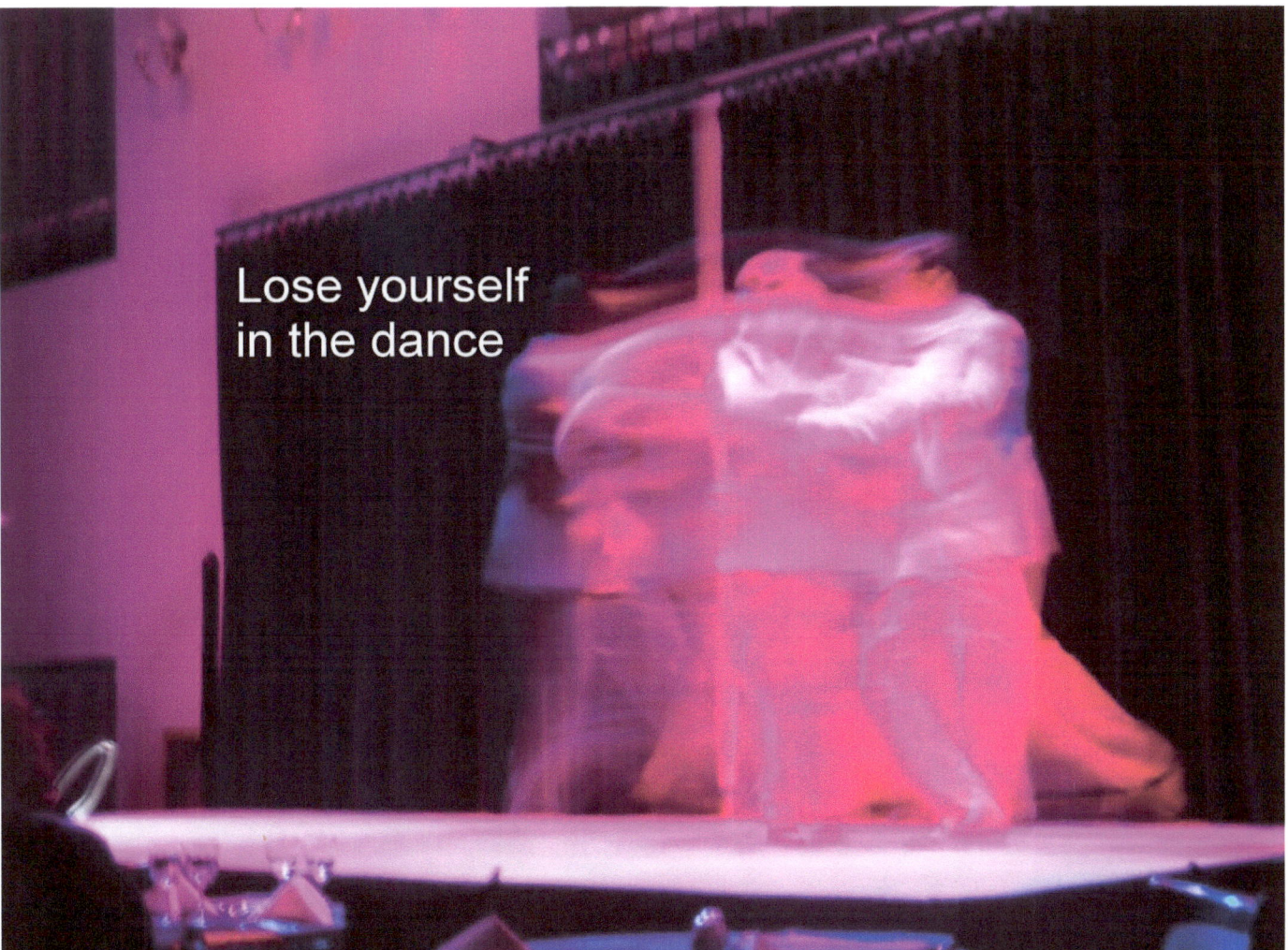

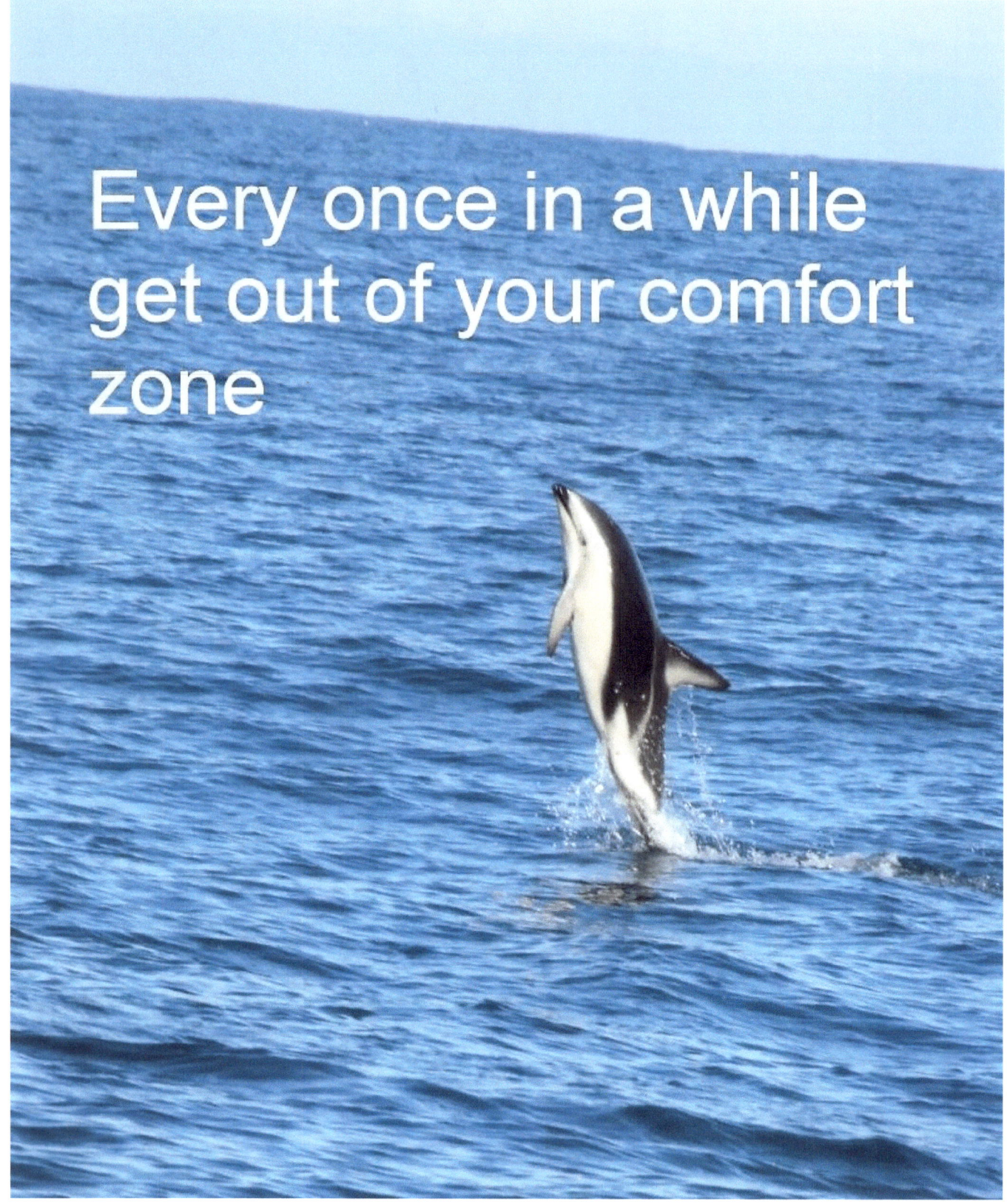

Every once in a while get out of your comfort zone

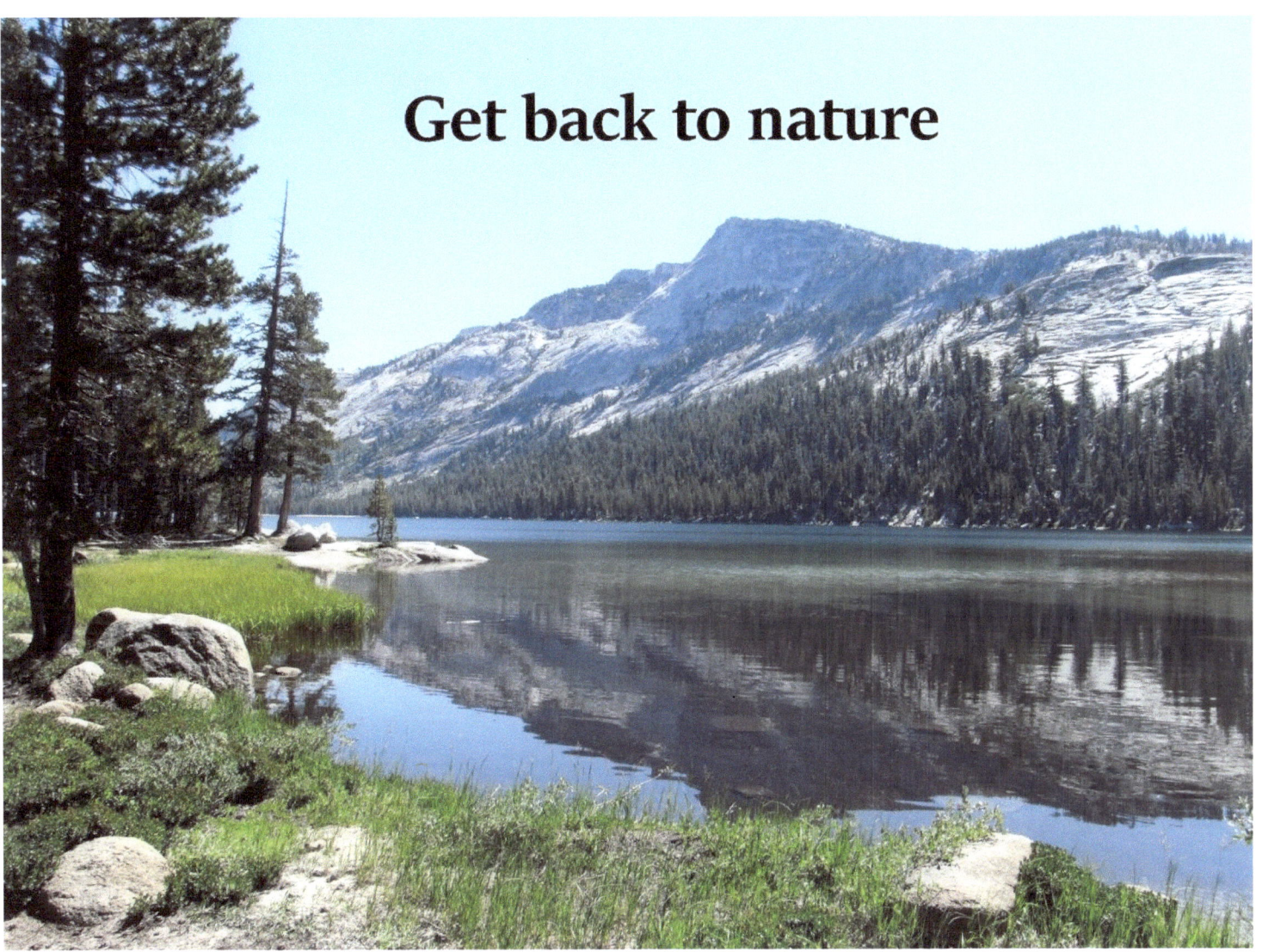

Get back to nature

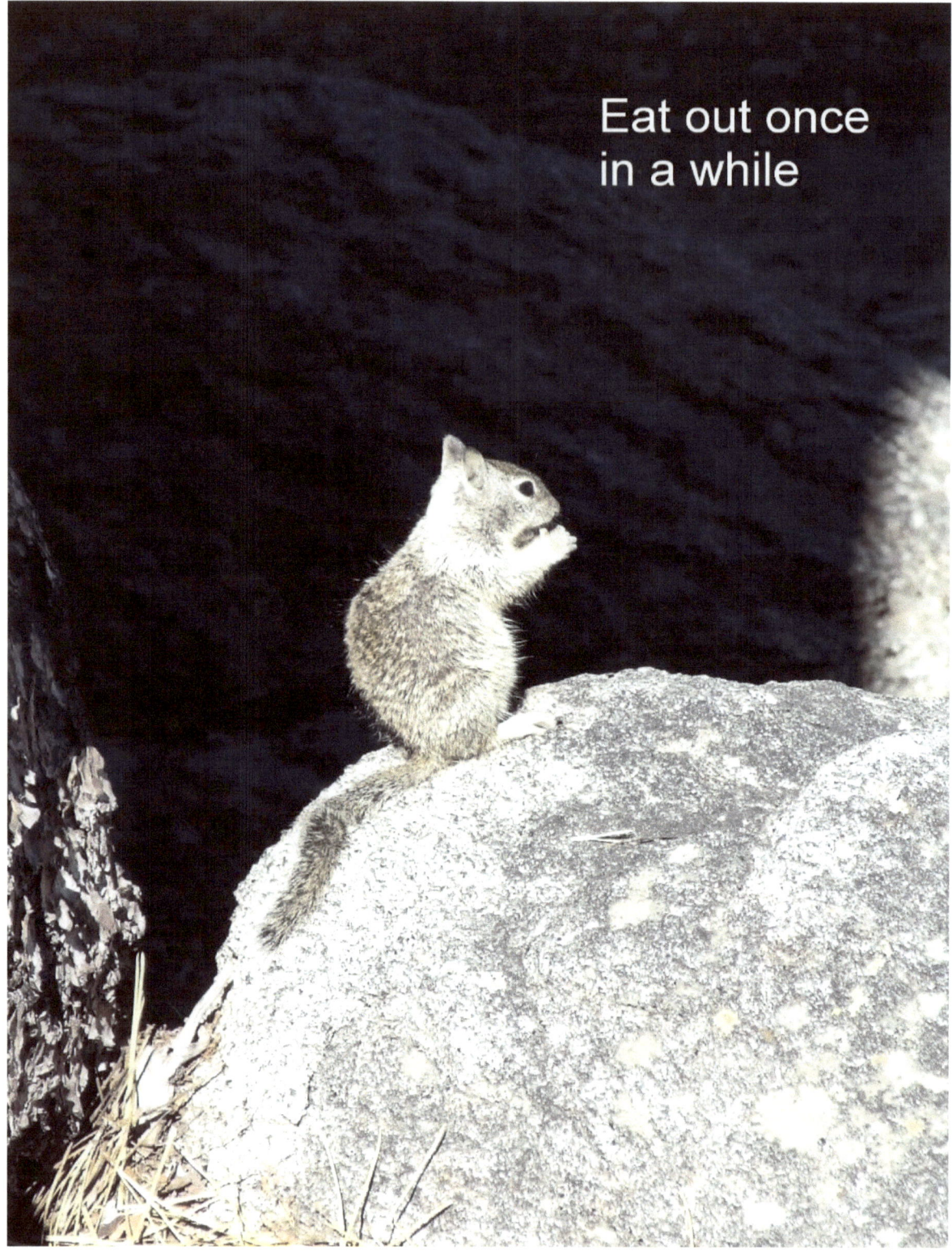

Eat out once
in a while

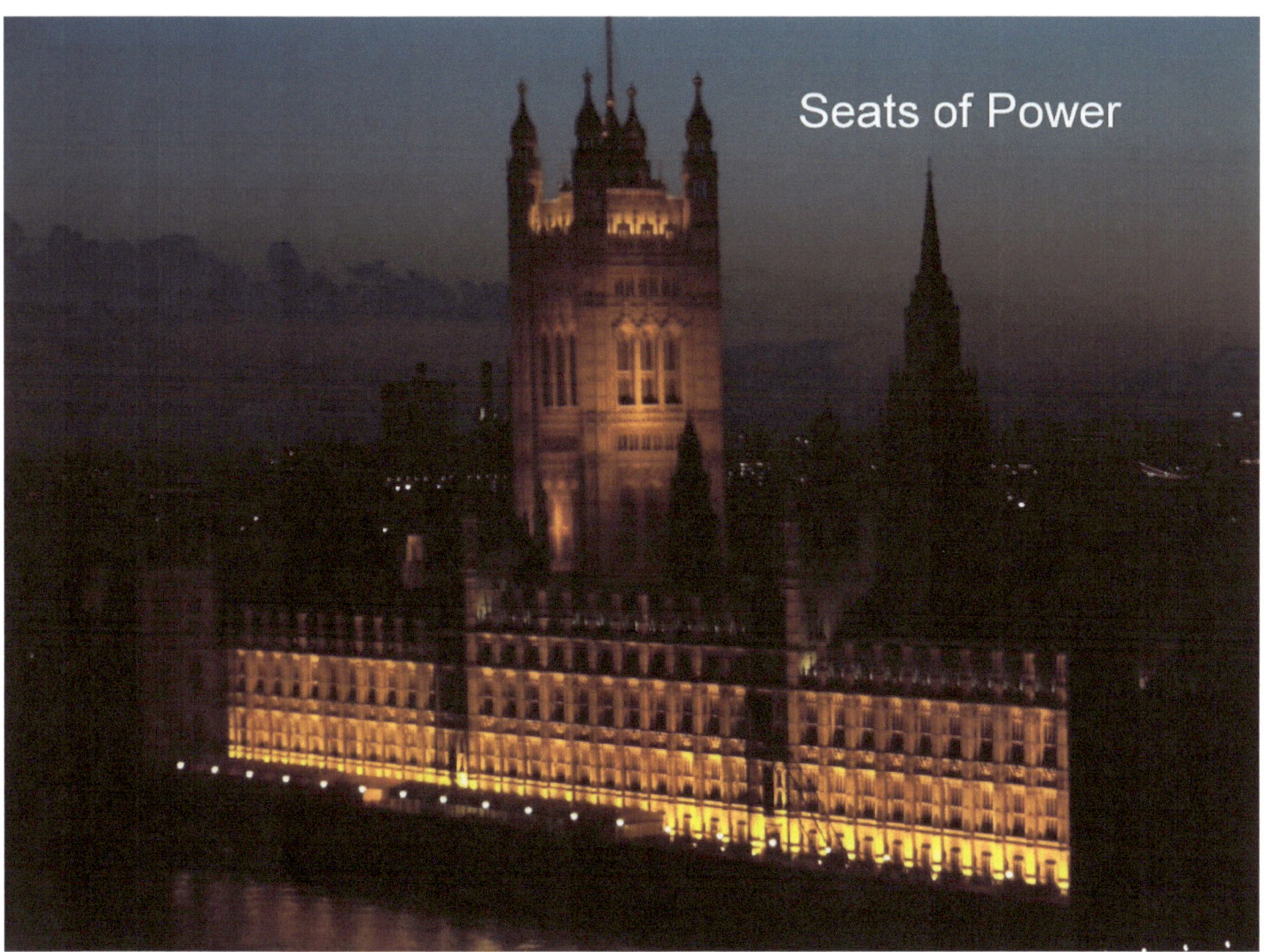

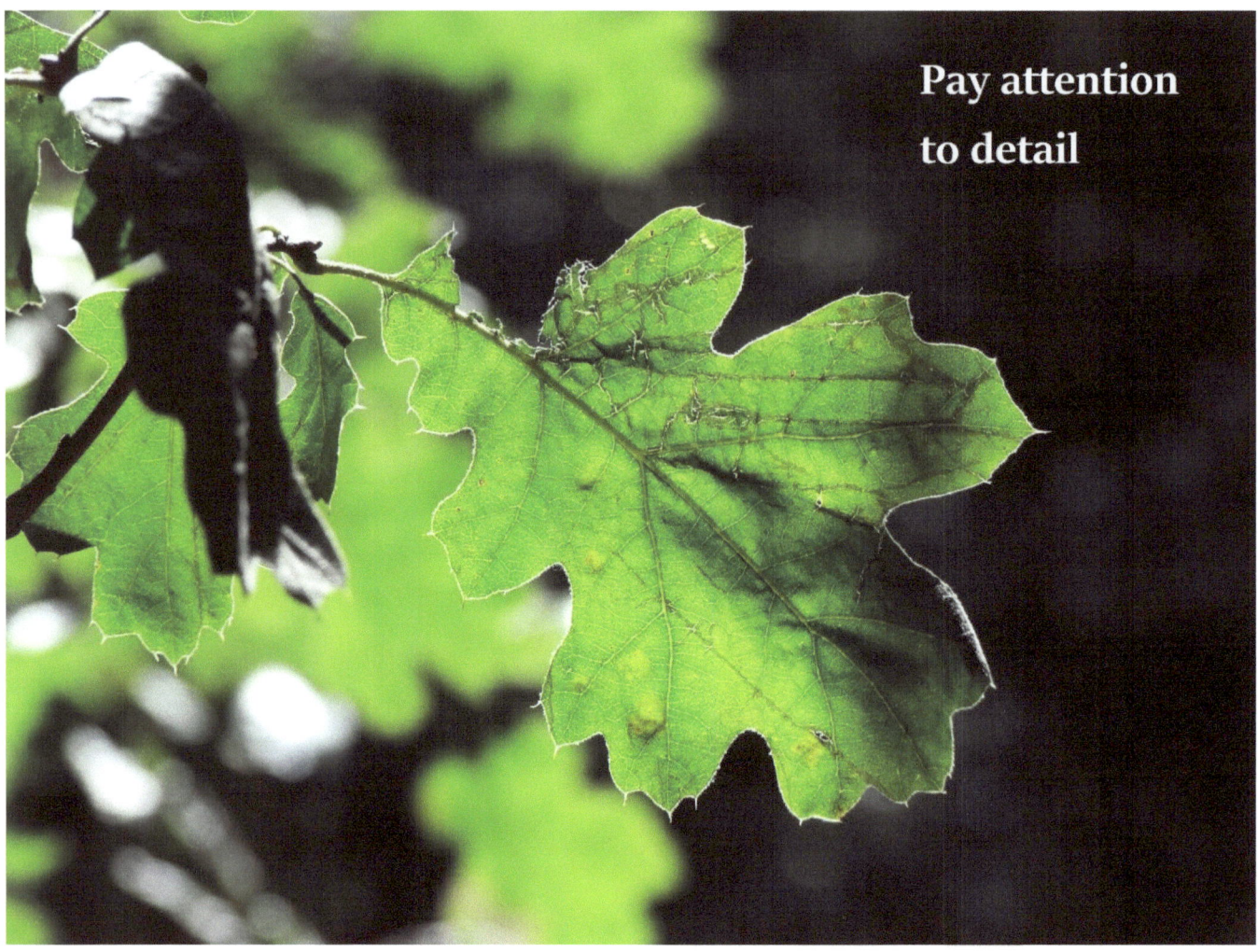

Pay attention to detail

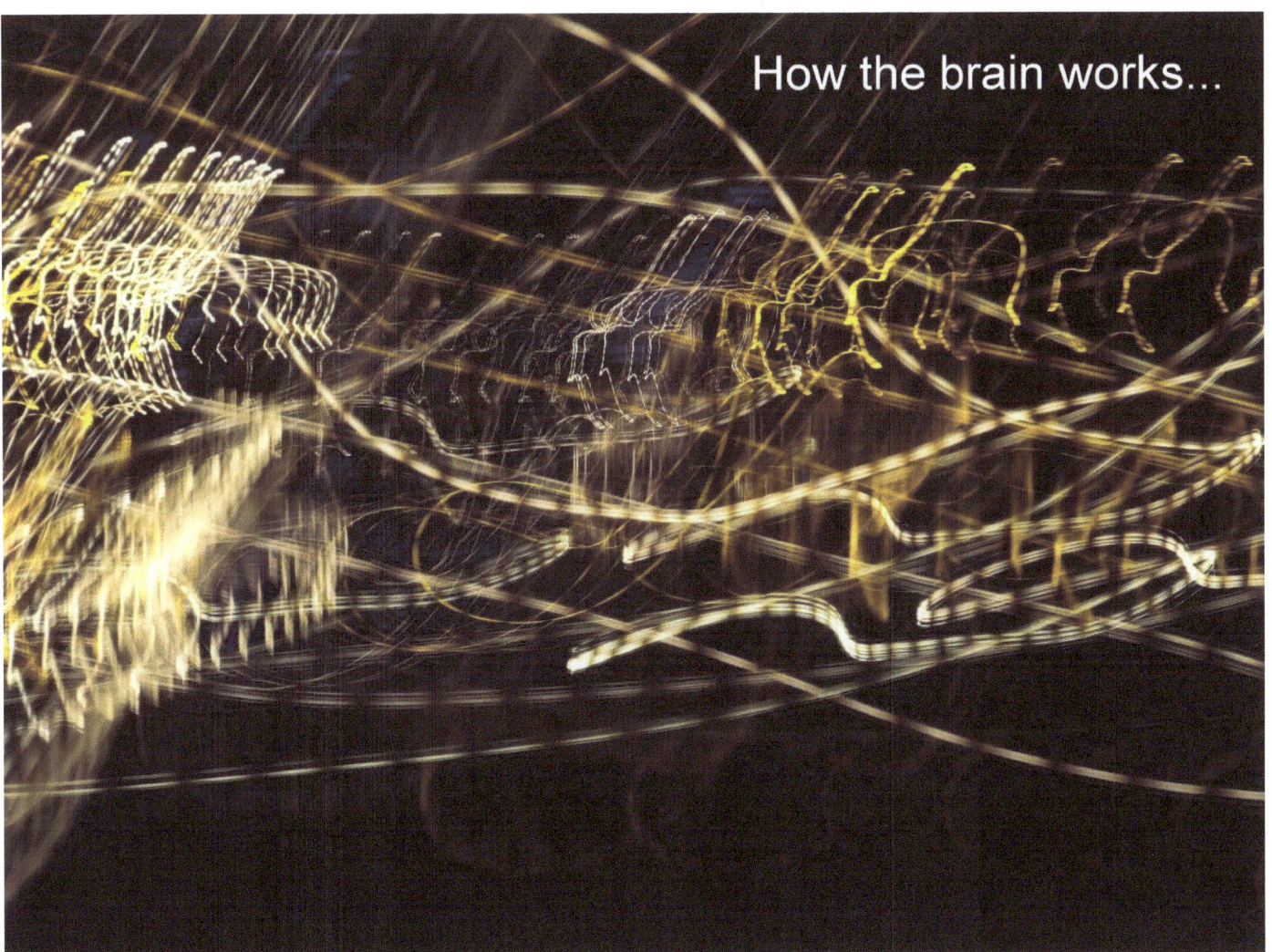

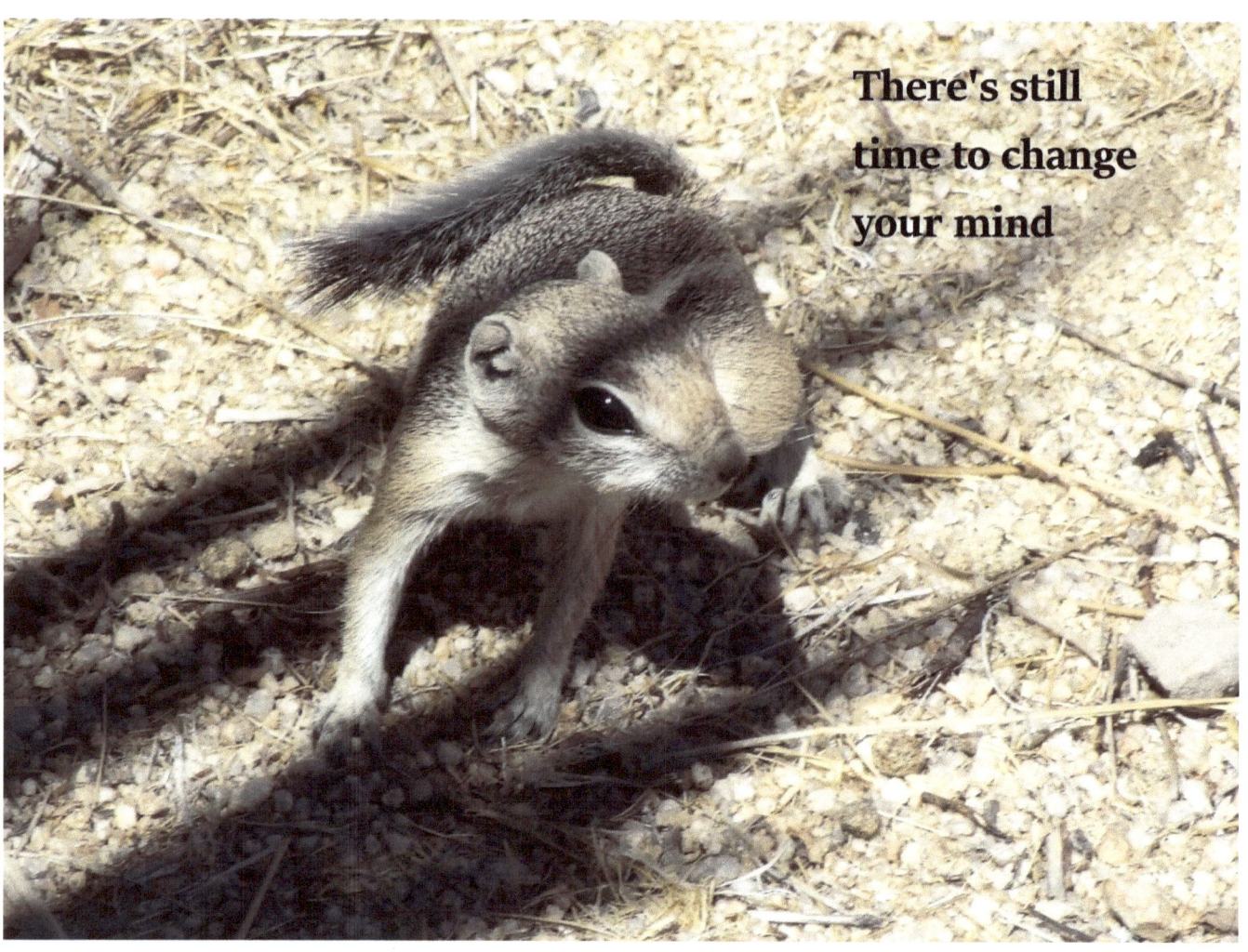

There's still time to change your mind

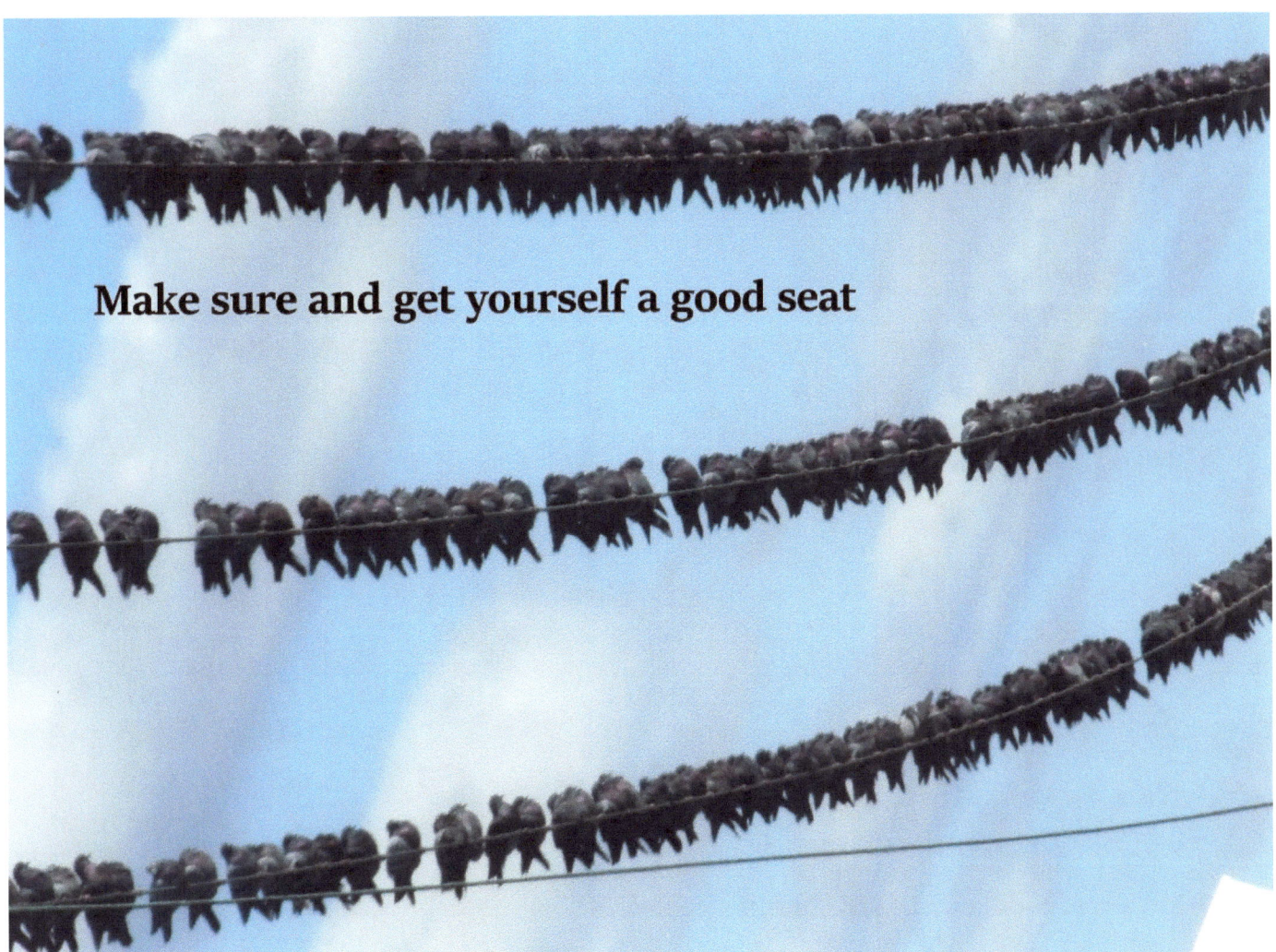

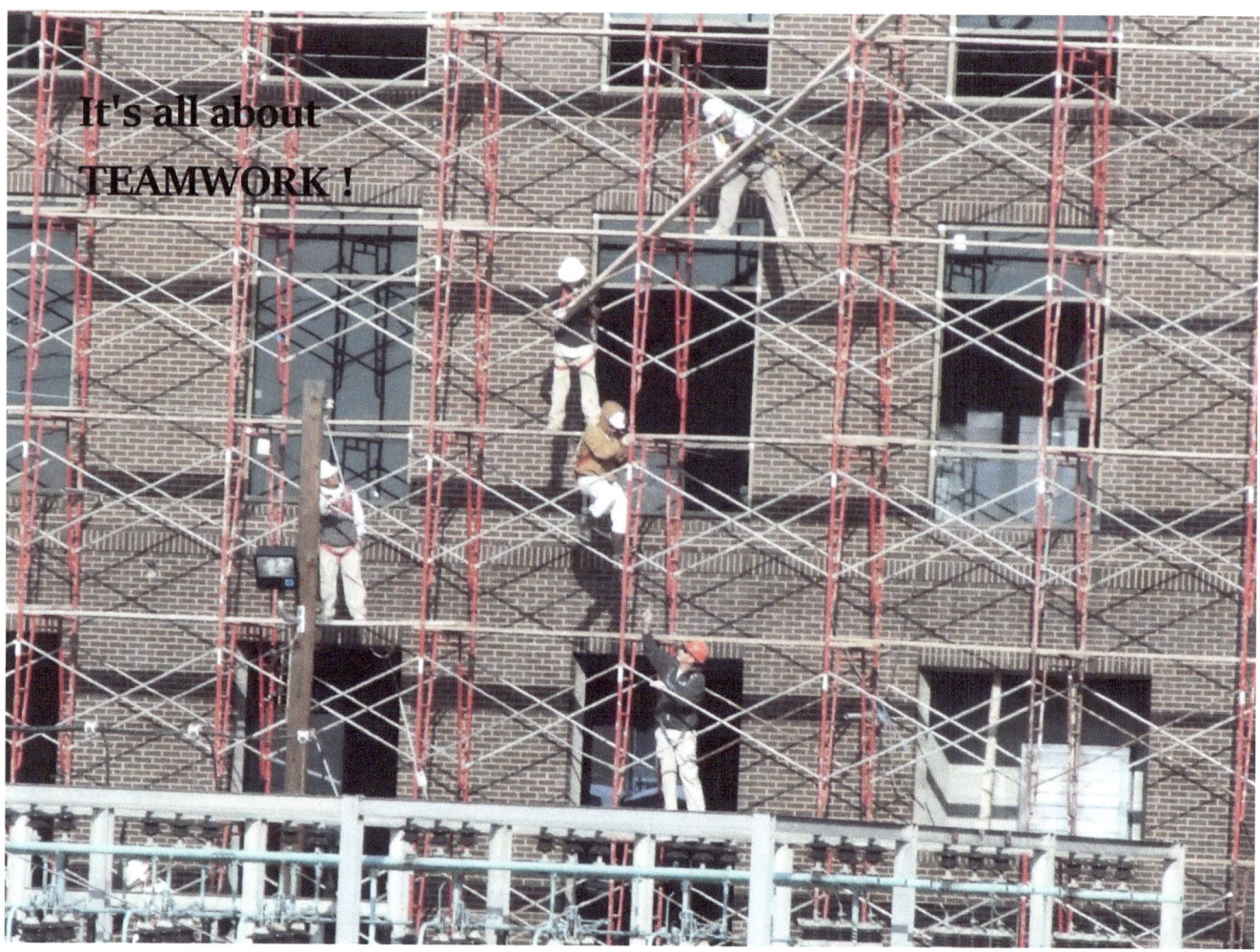

It's all about
TEAMWORK !

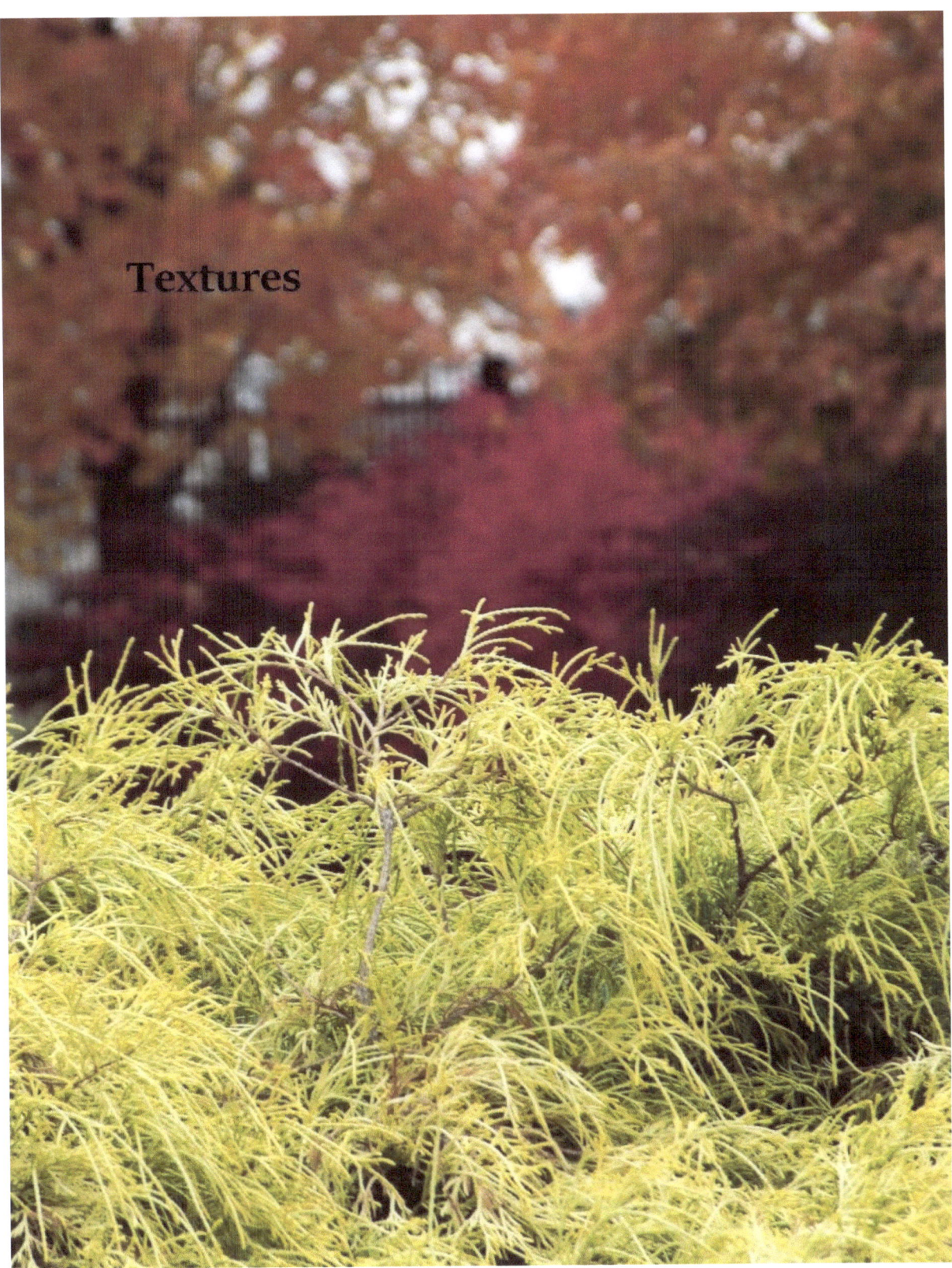

Textures

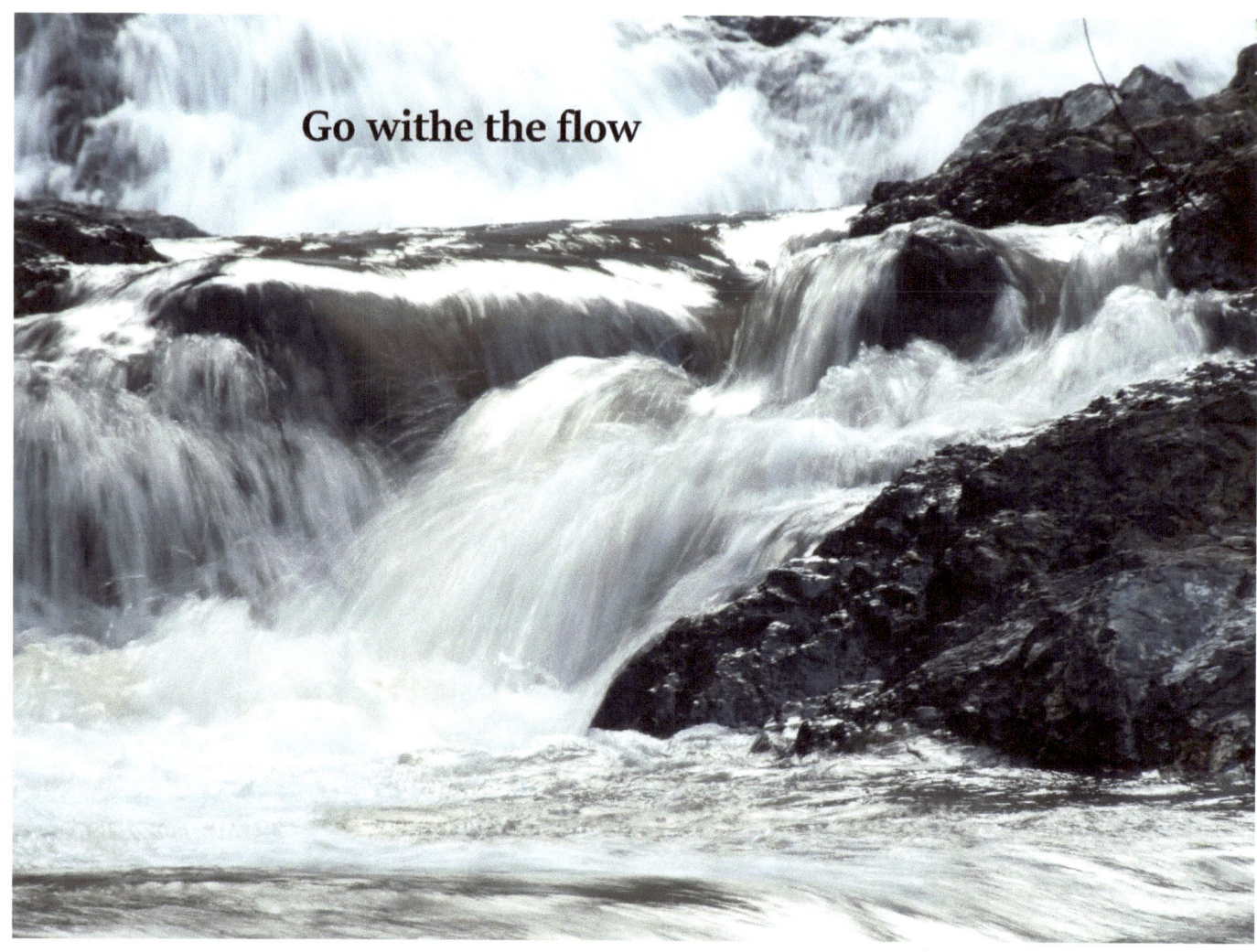

Go withe the flow

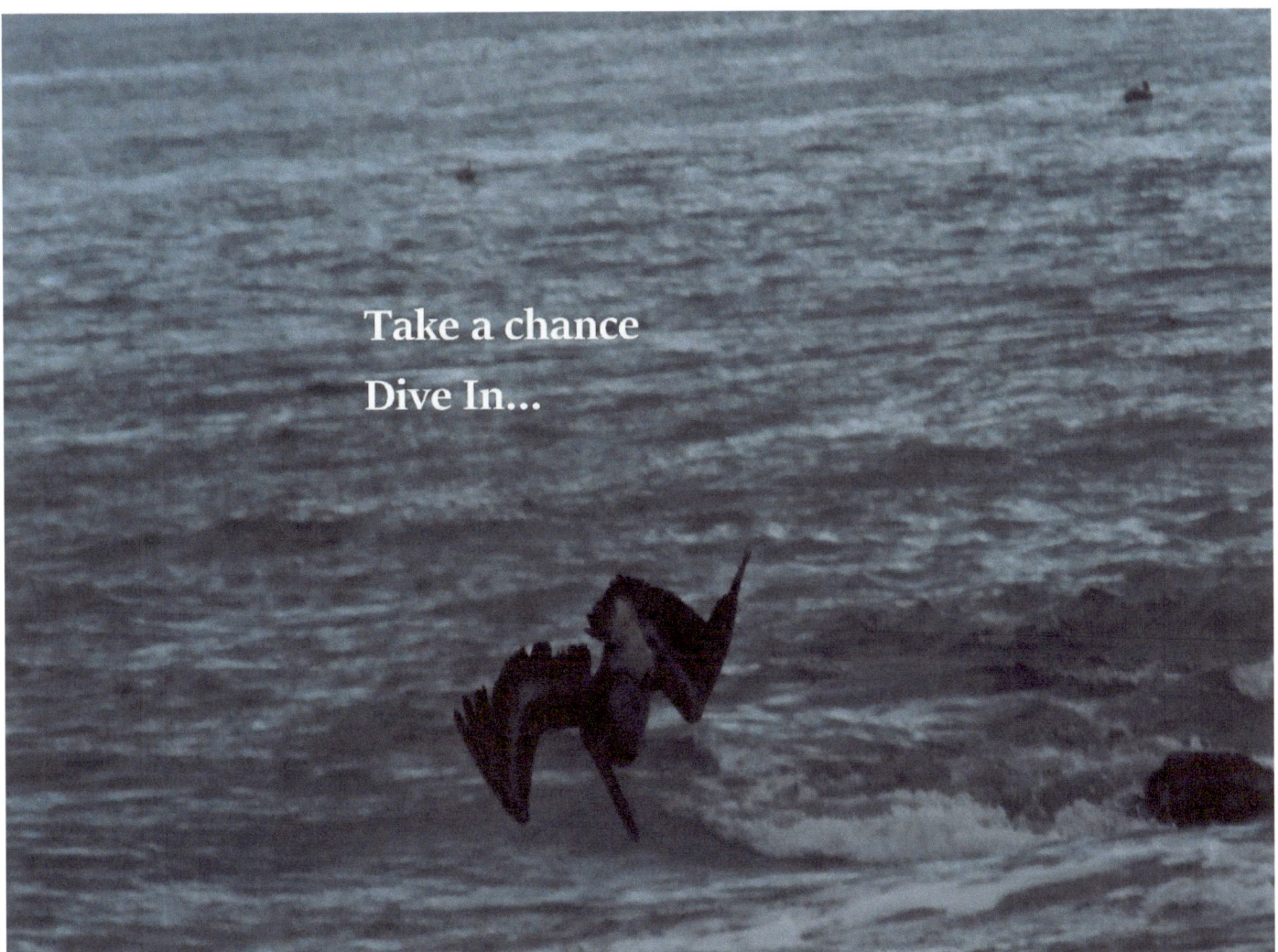

Take a chance

Dive In...

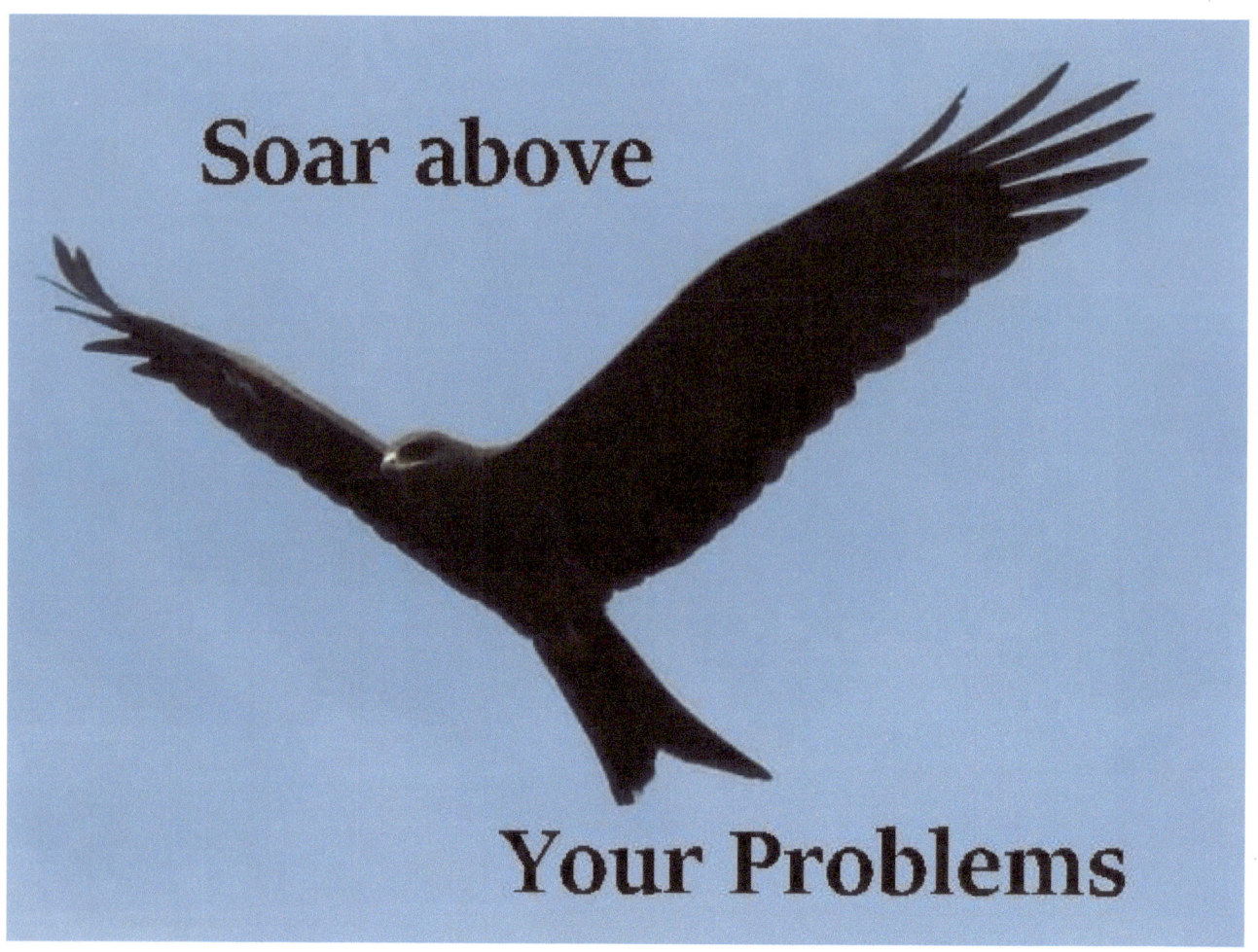

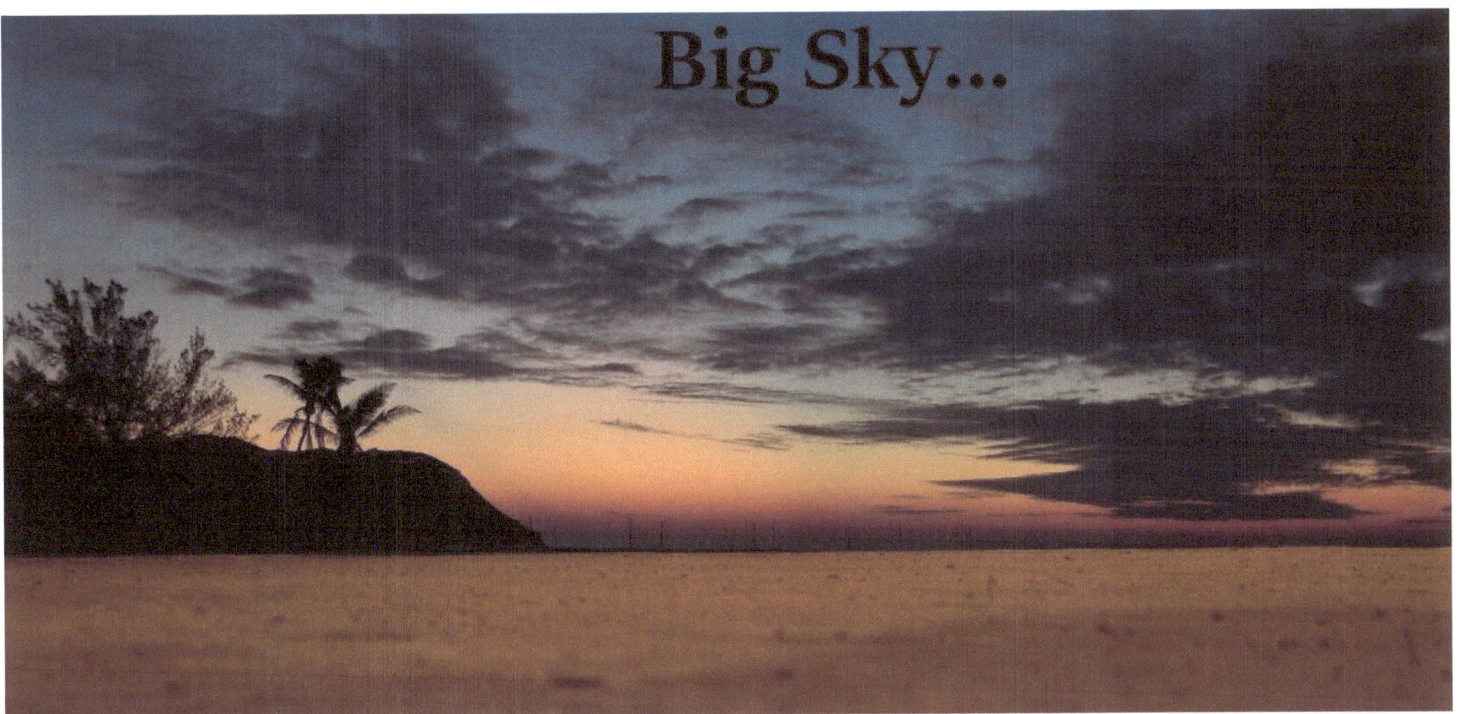

Big Sky...

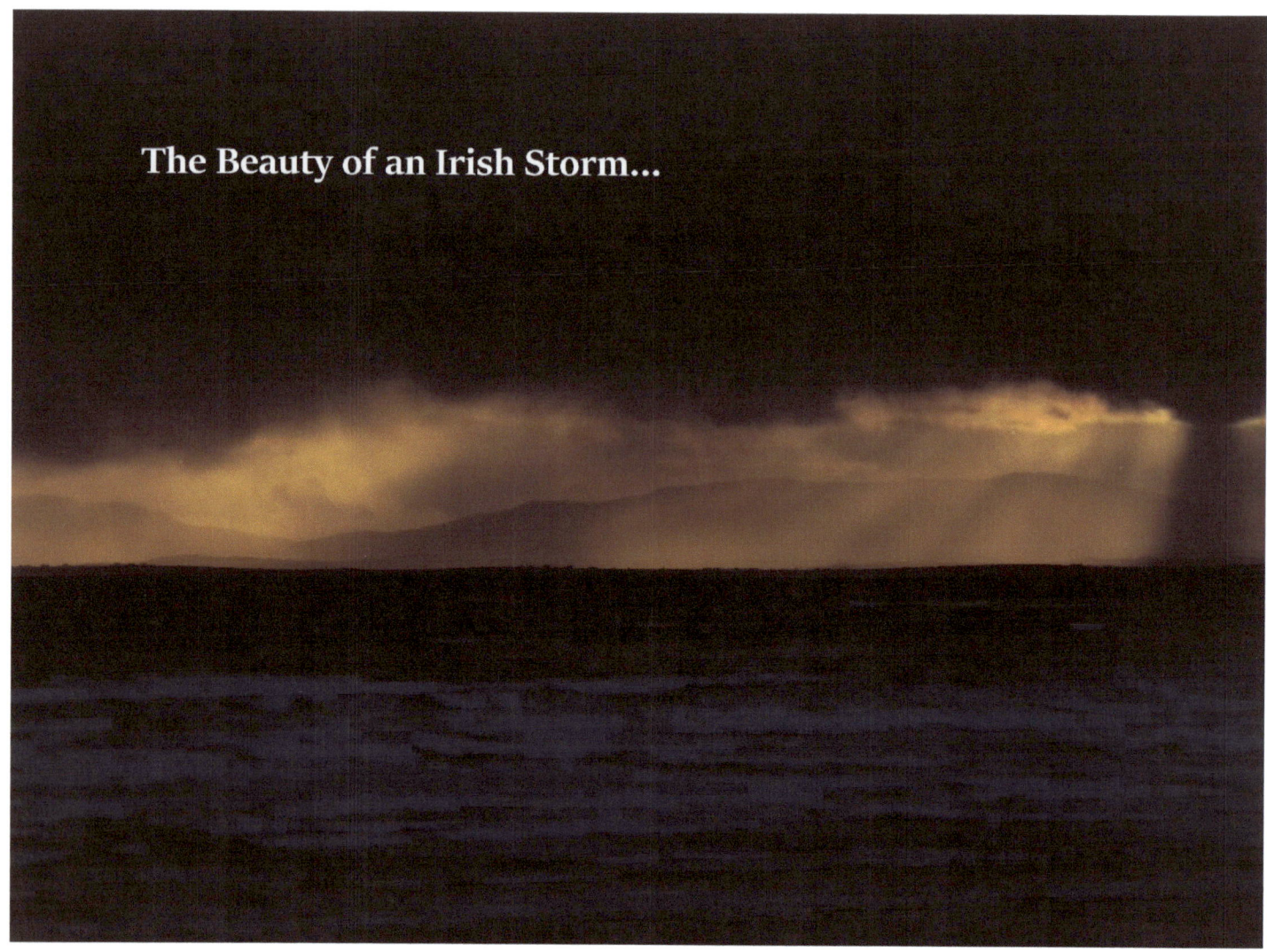

The Beauty of an Irish Storm...

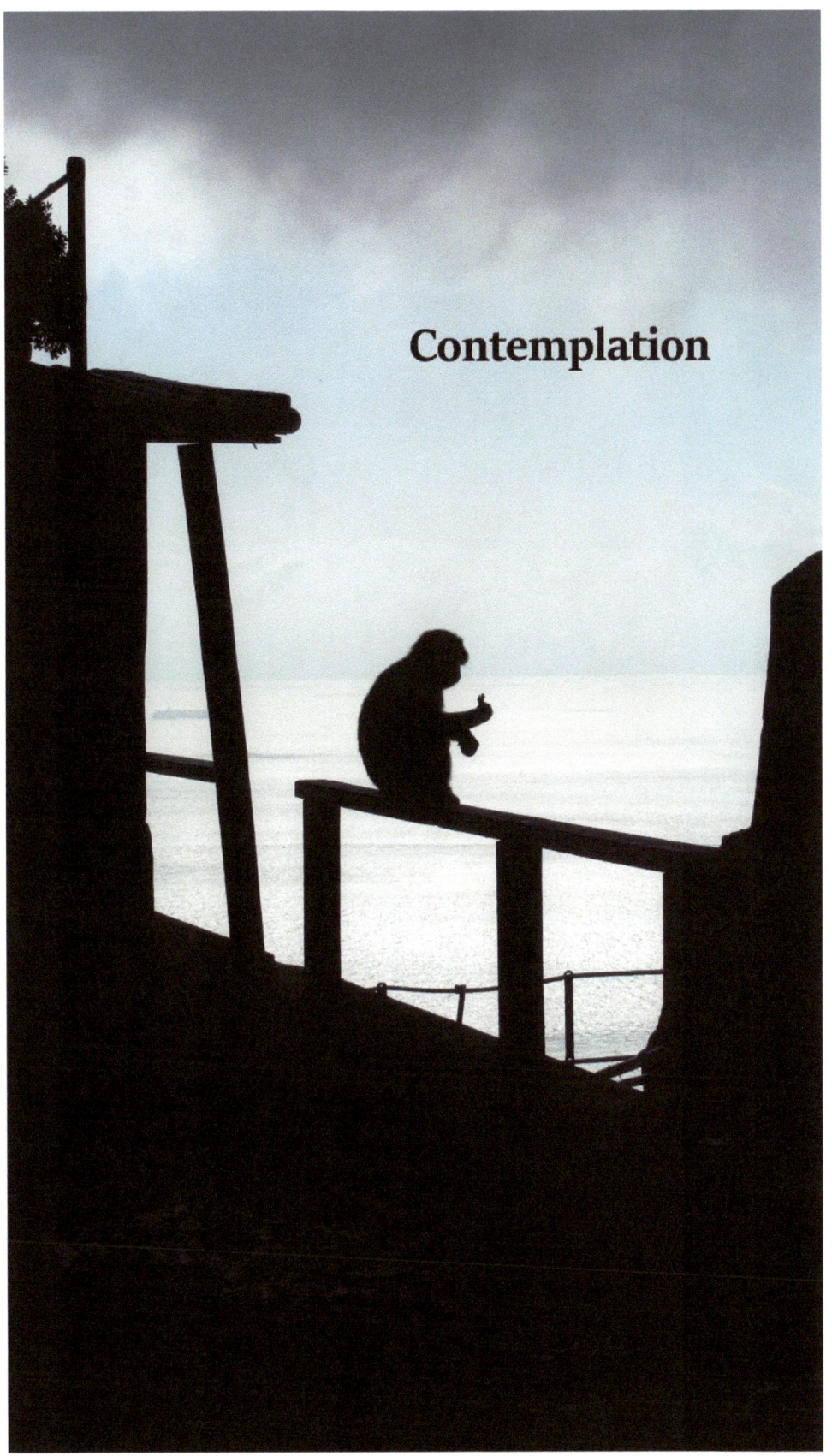

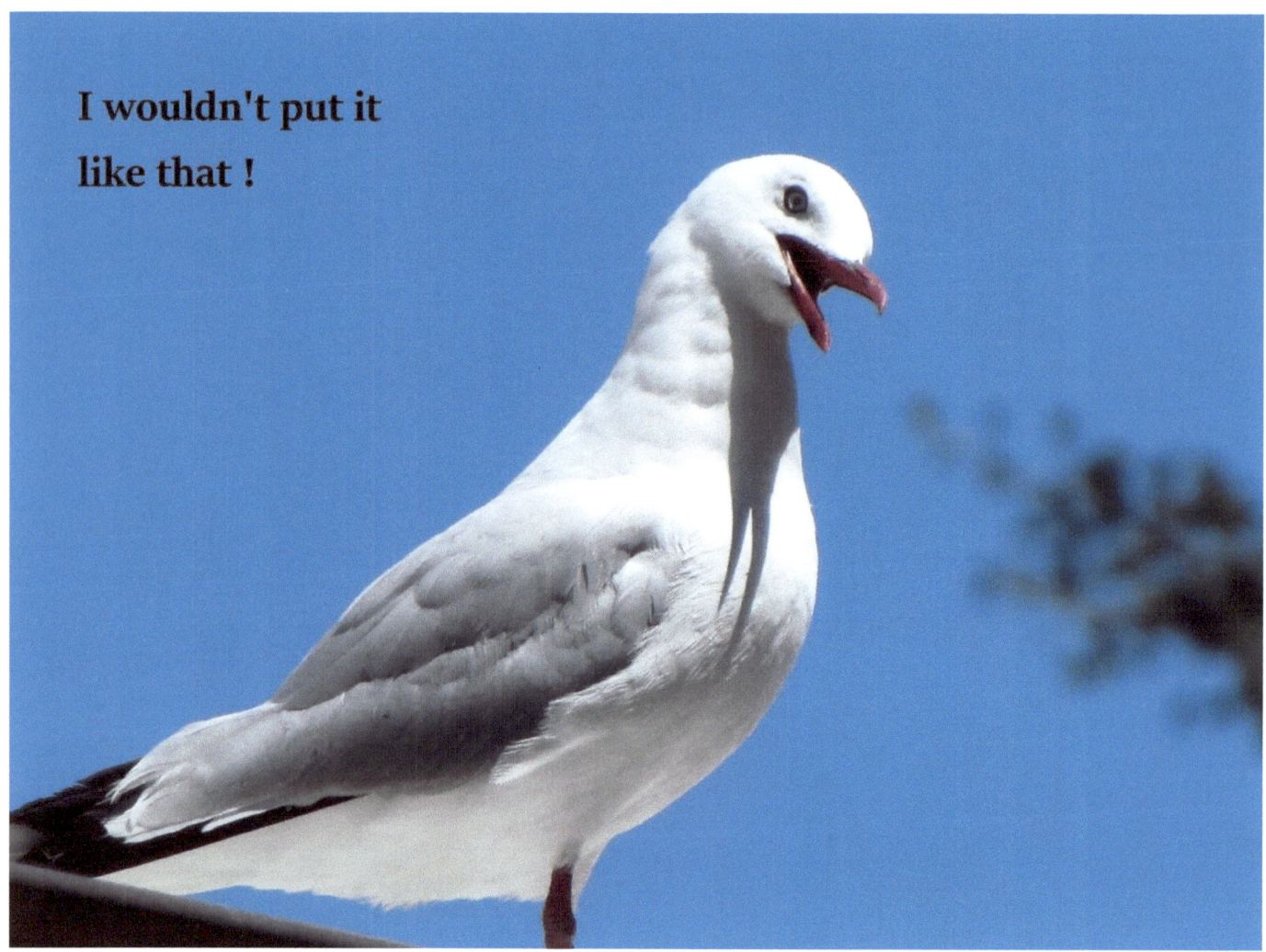

I wouldn't put it
like that !

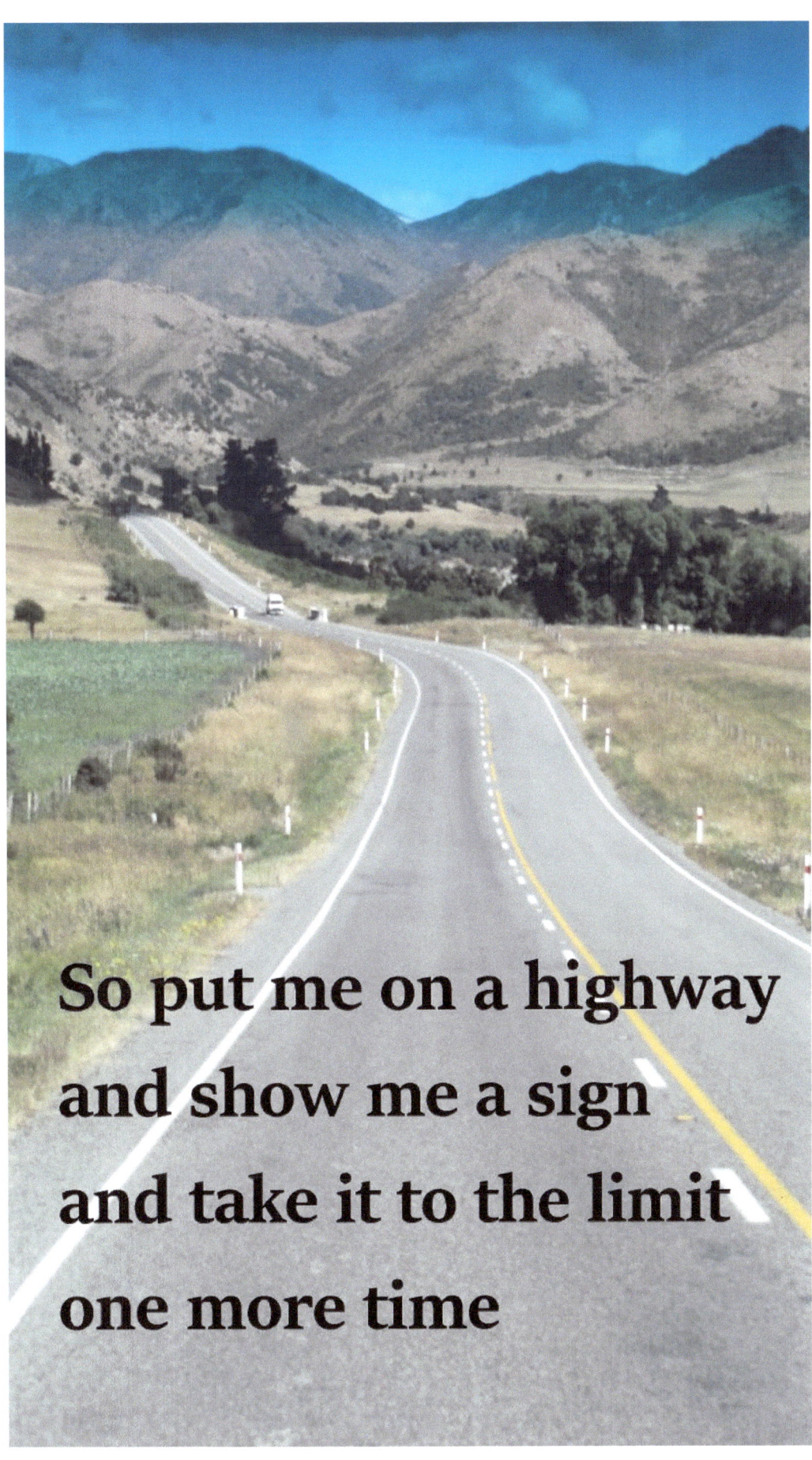

So put me on a highway
and show me a sign
and take it to the limit
one more time

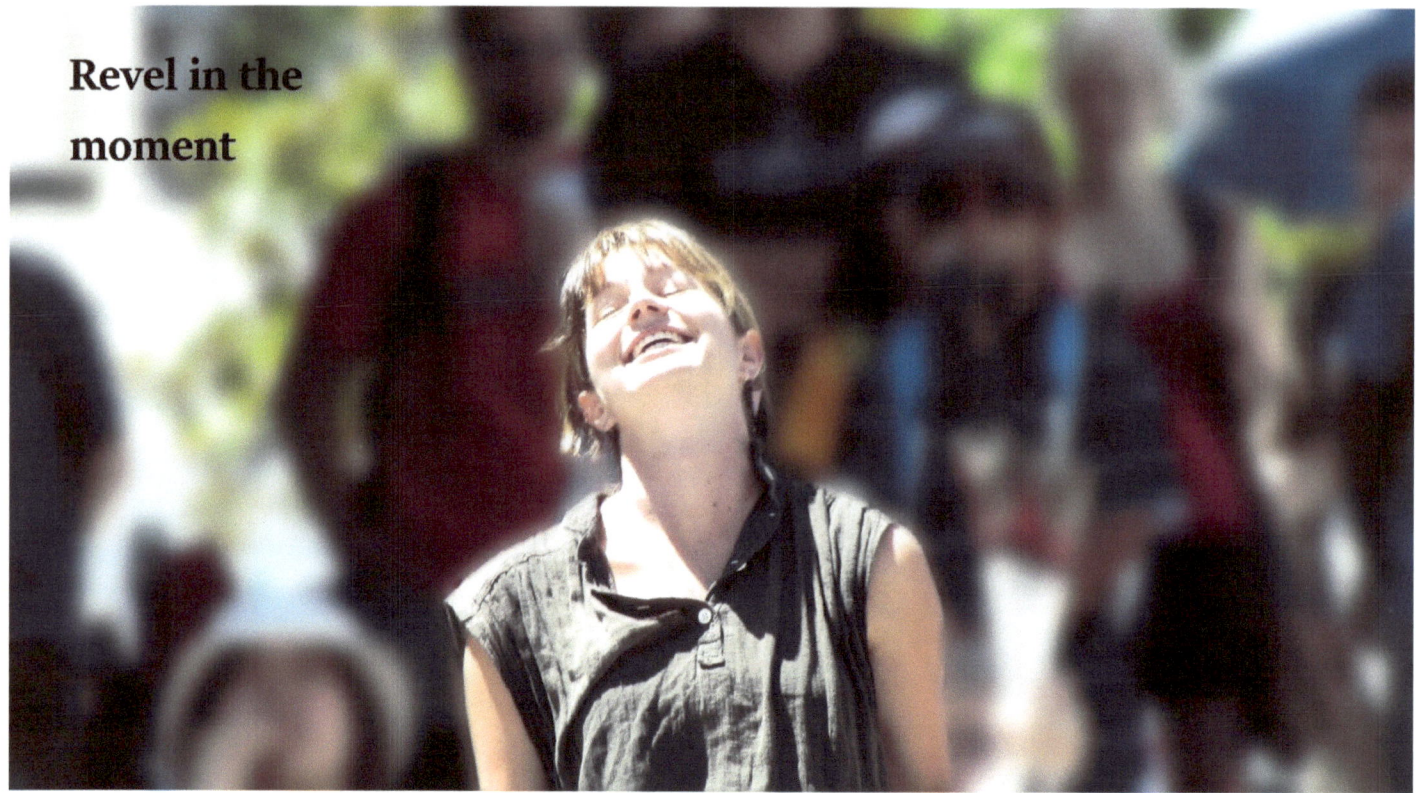

Revel in the moment

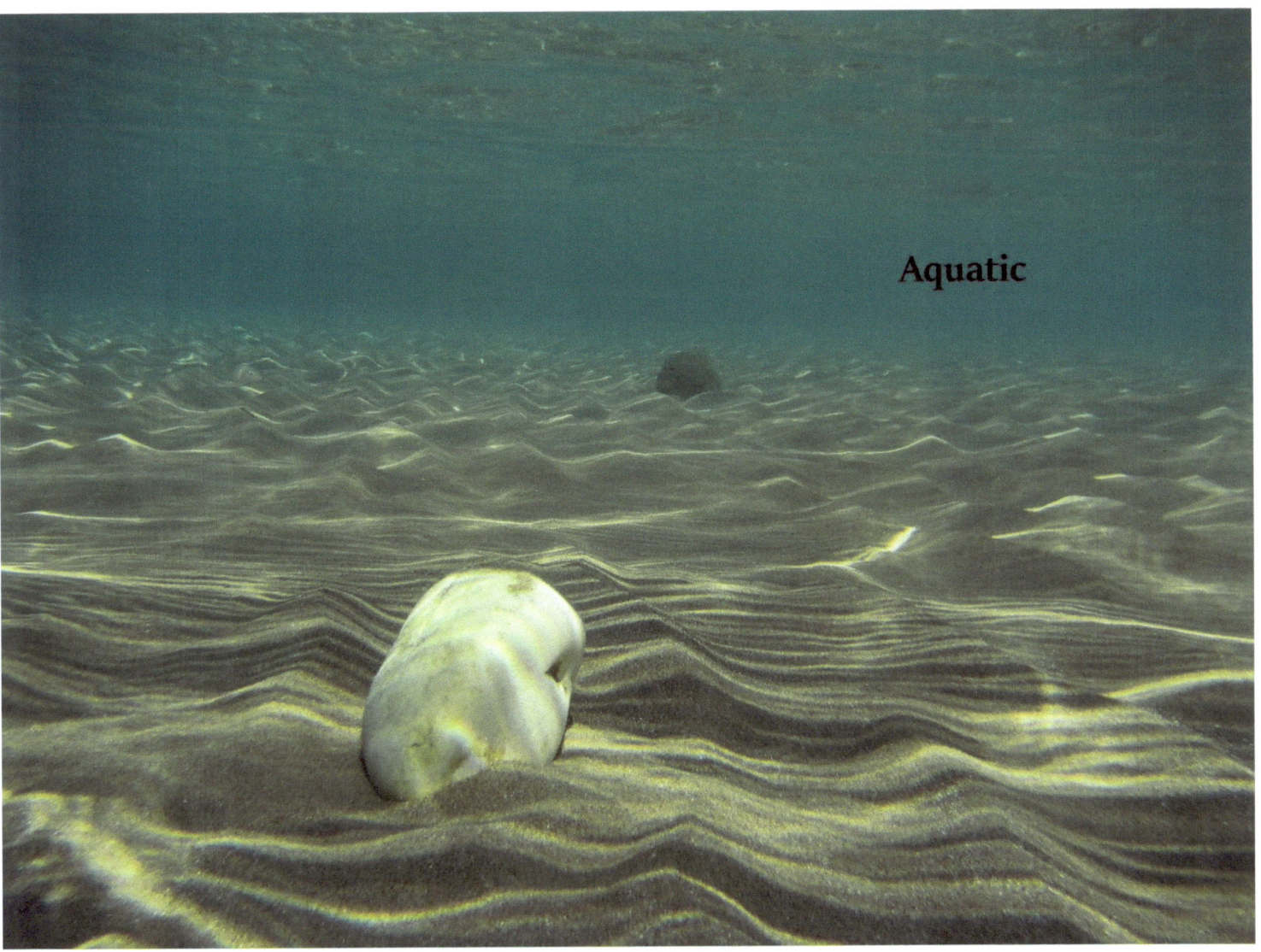

Aquatic

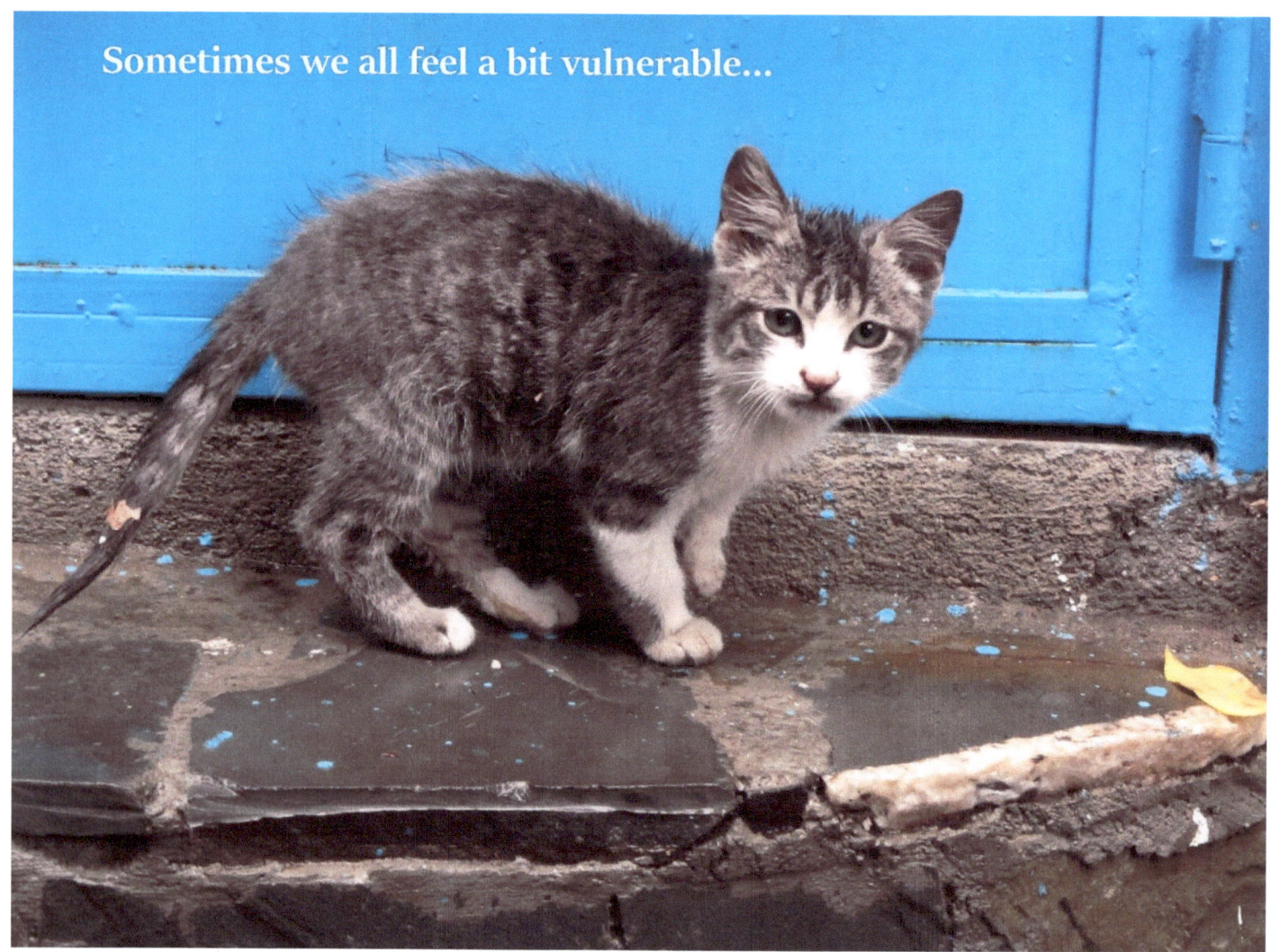

Sometimes we all feel a bit vulnerable...

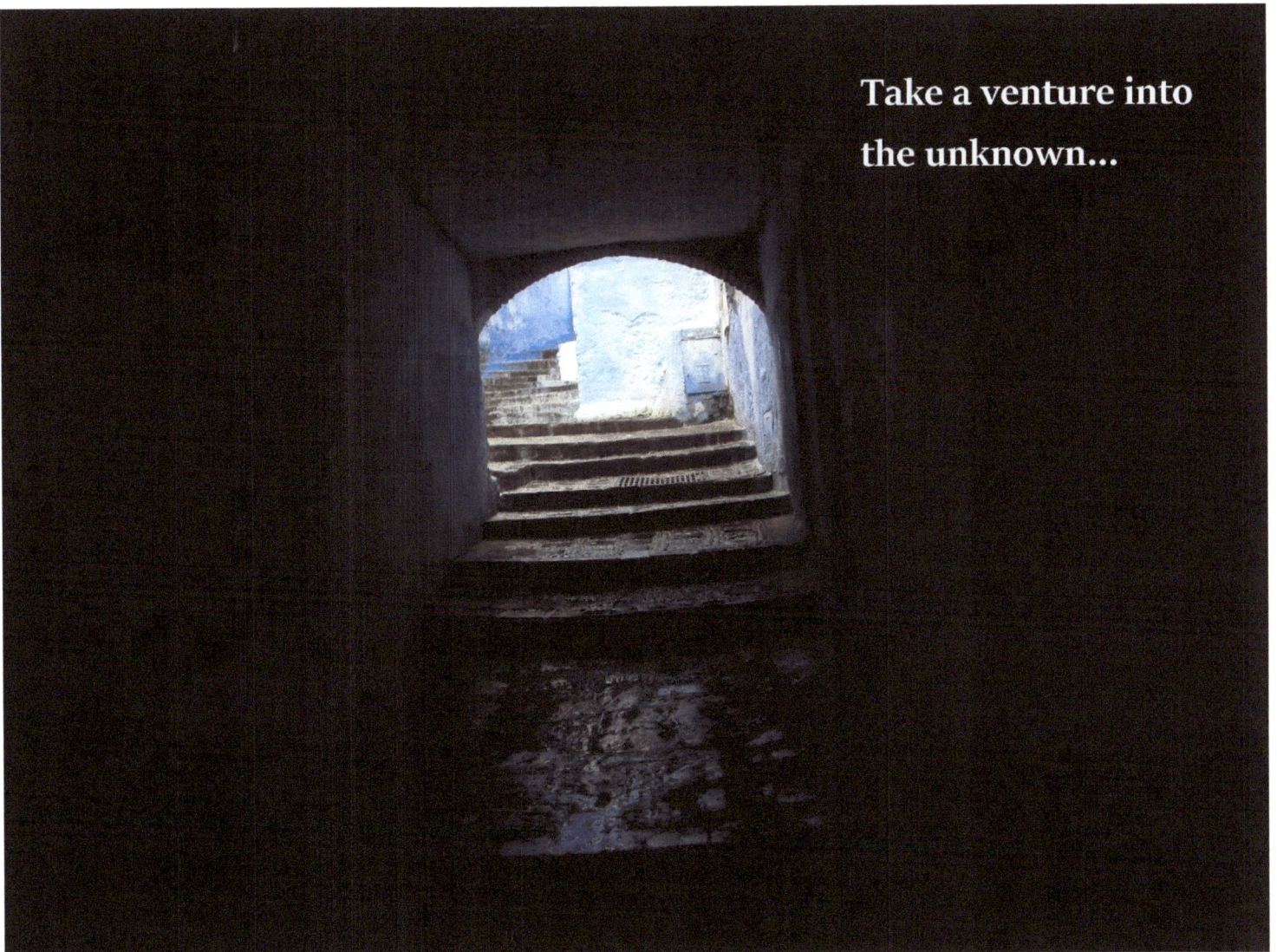

Take a venture into
the unknown...

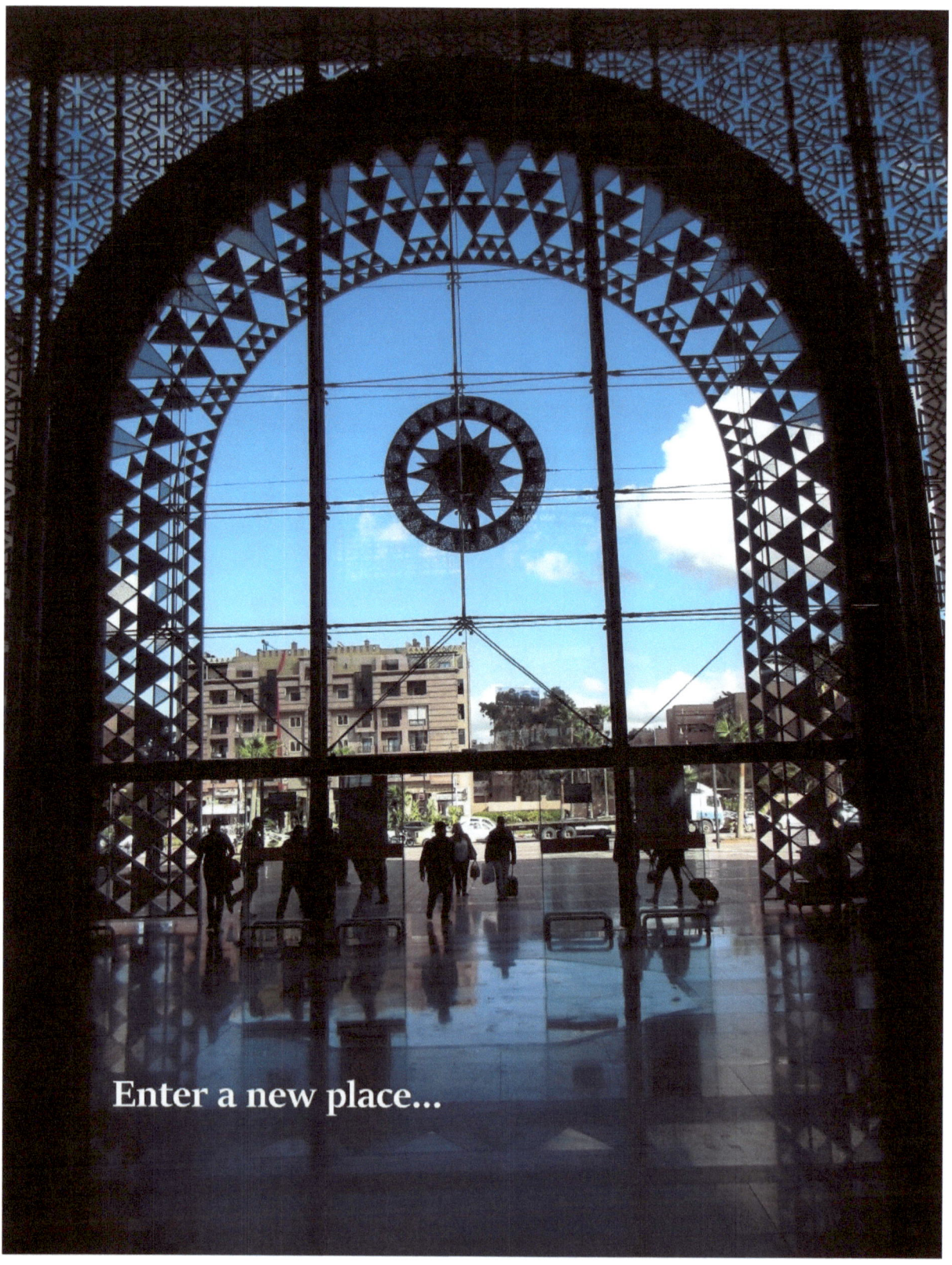

Enter a new place...

Take stock of your kingdom

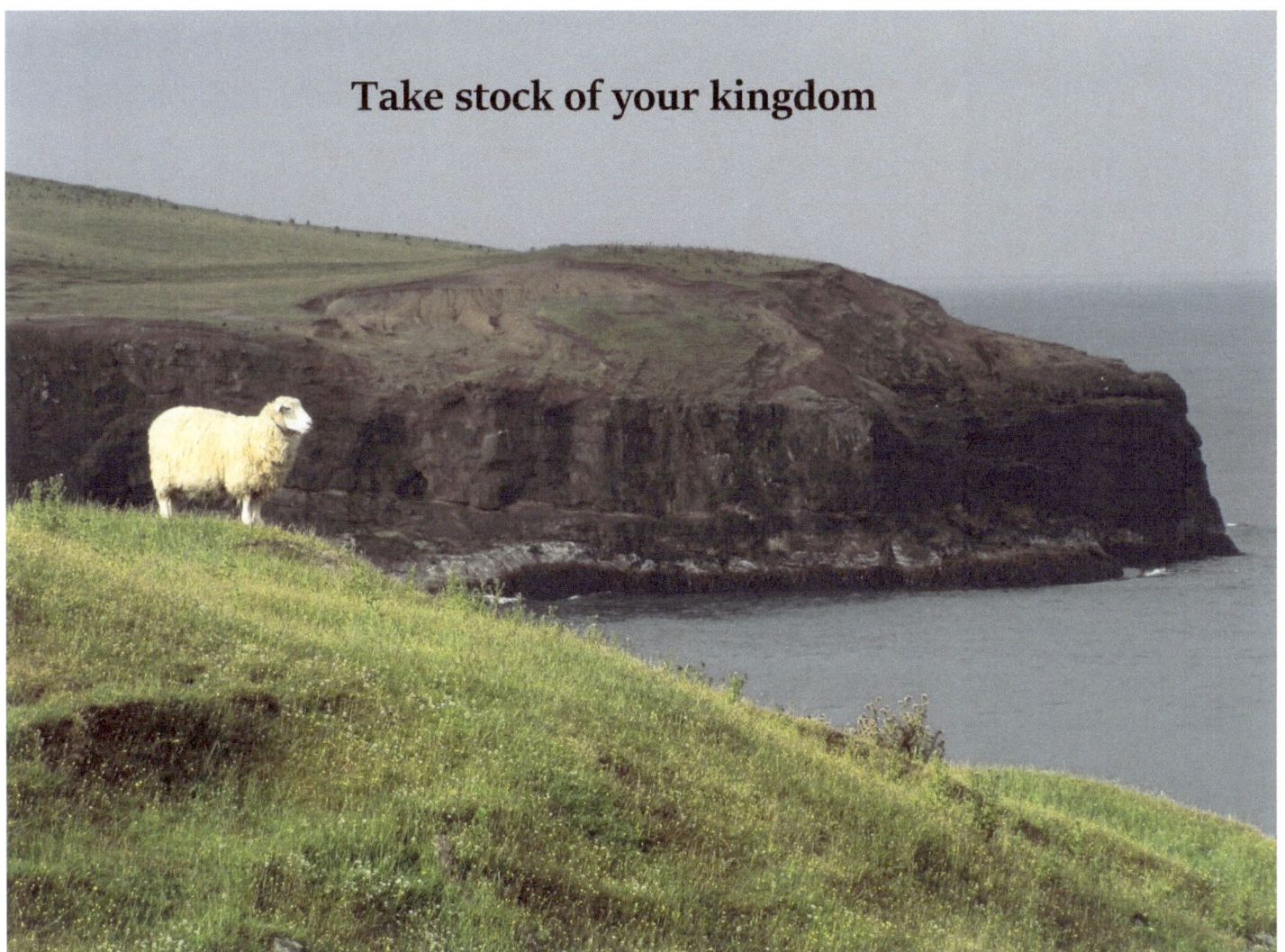

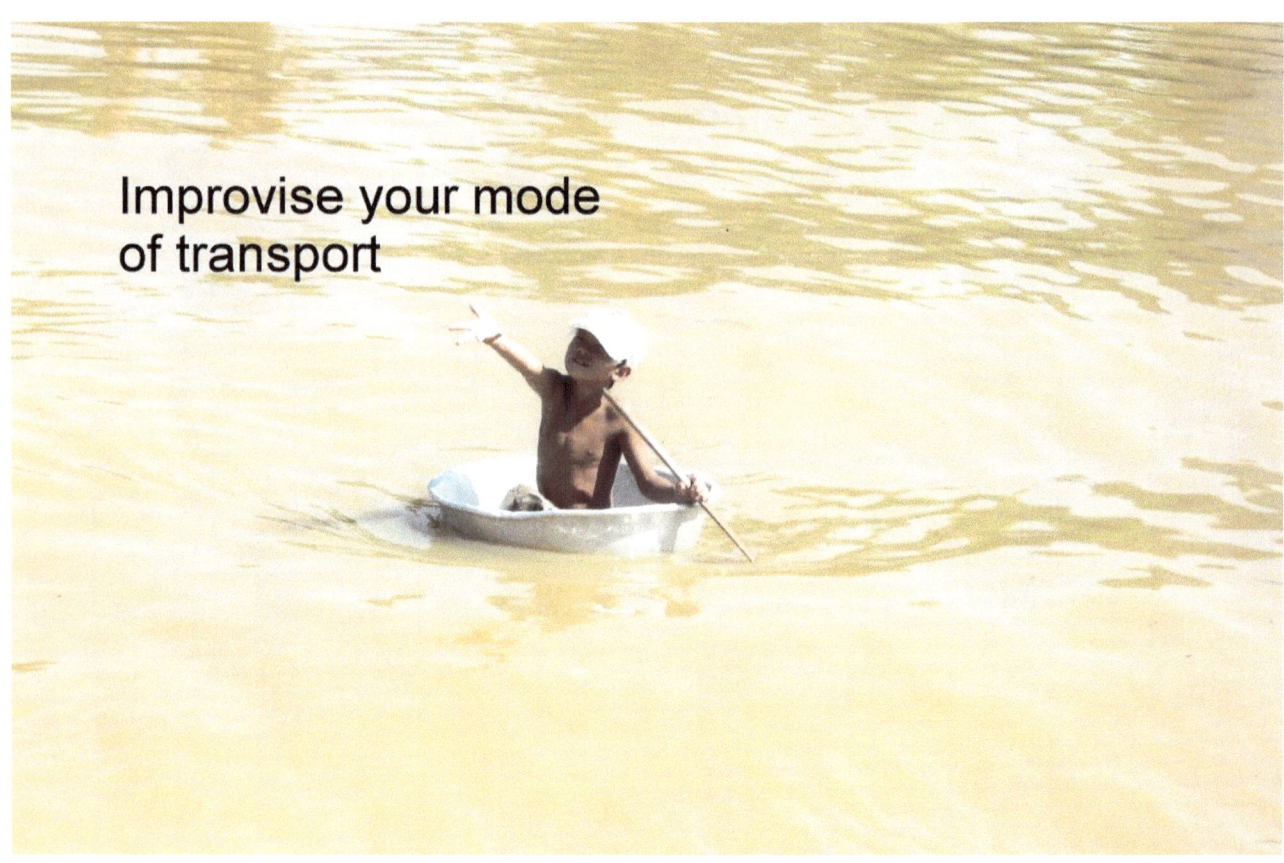

Improvise your mode
of transport

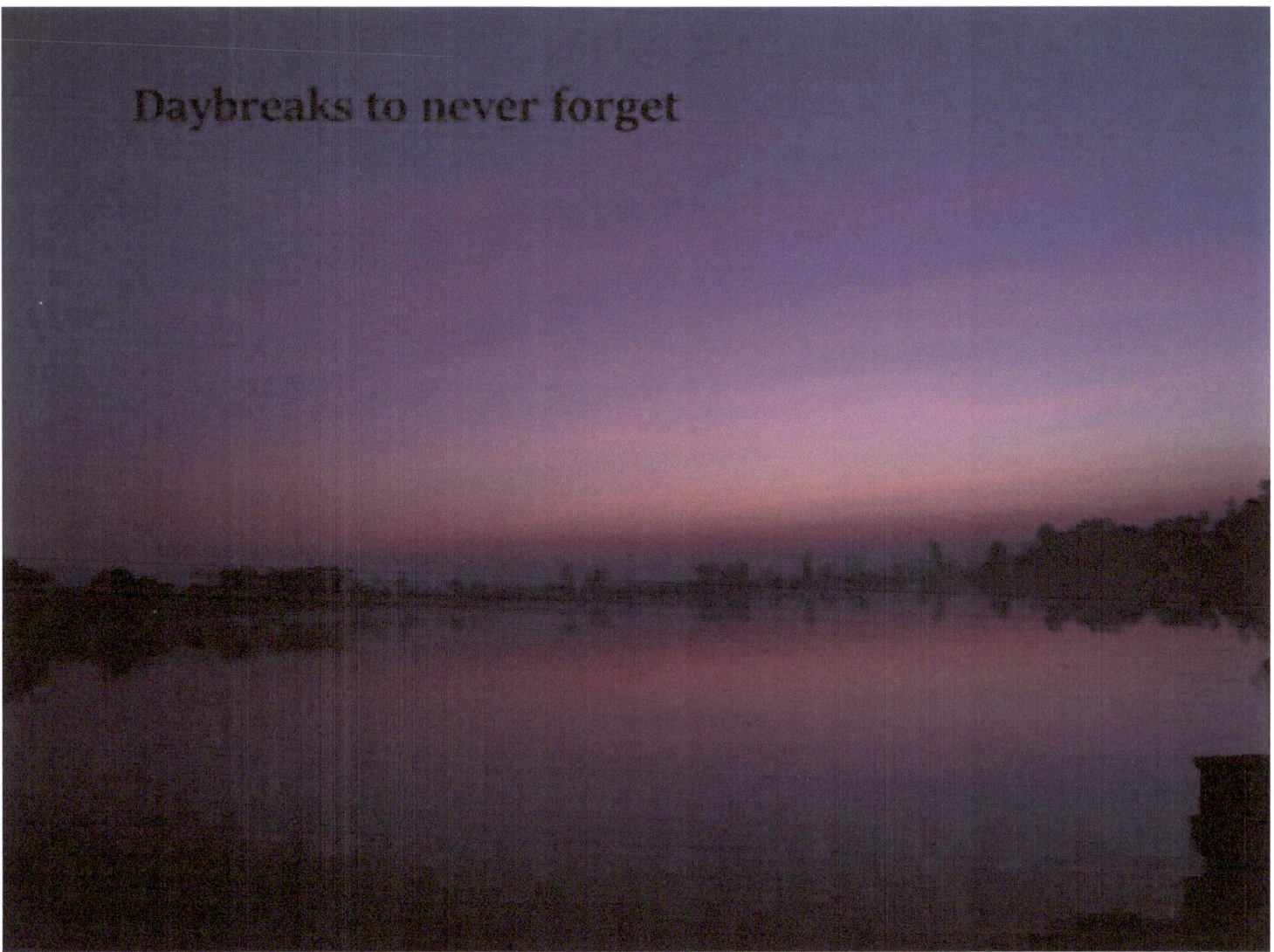

Daybreaks to never forget

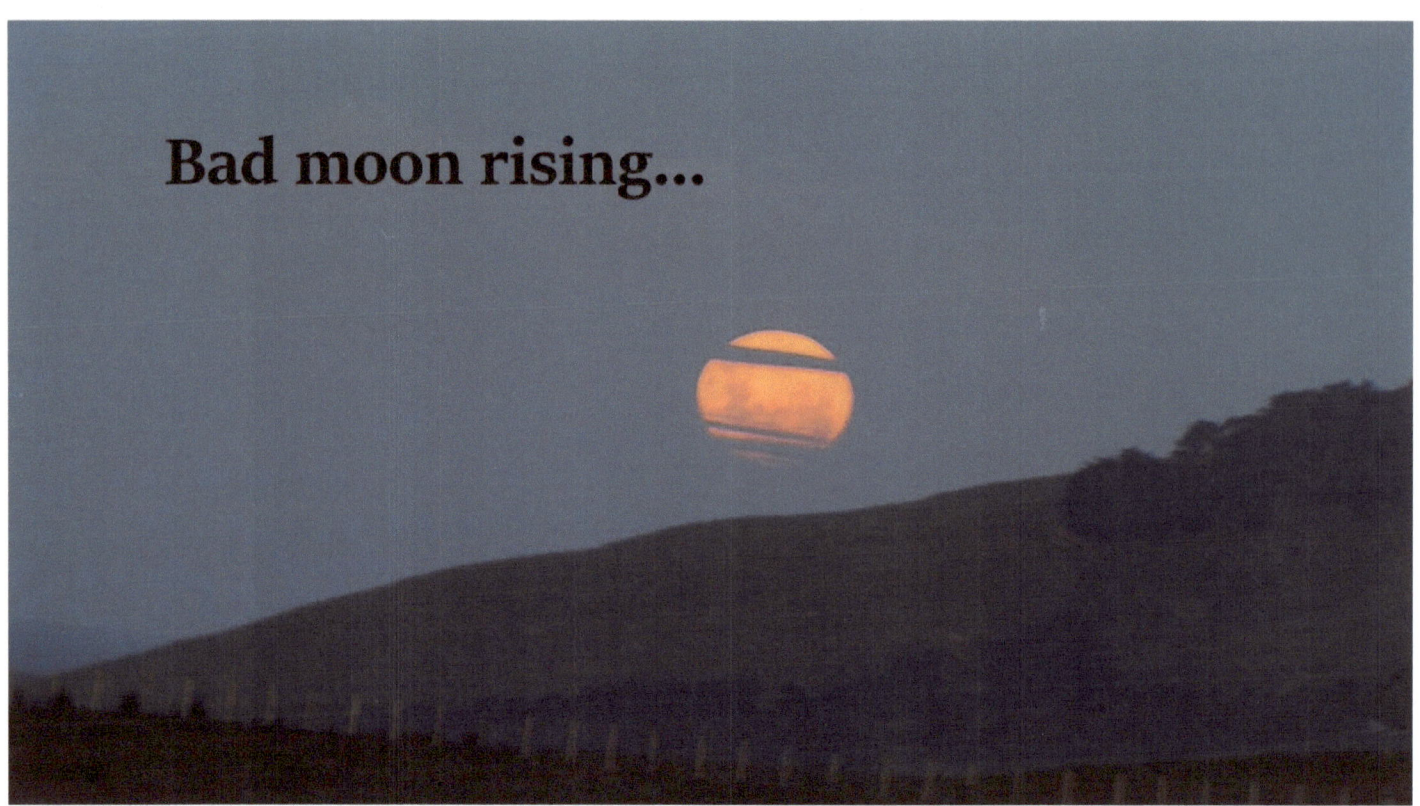

Bad moon rising...

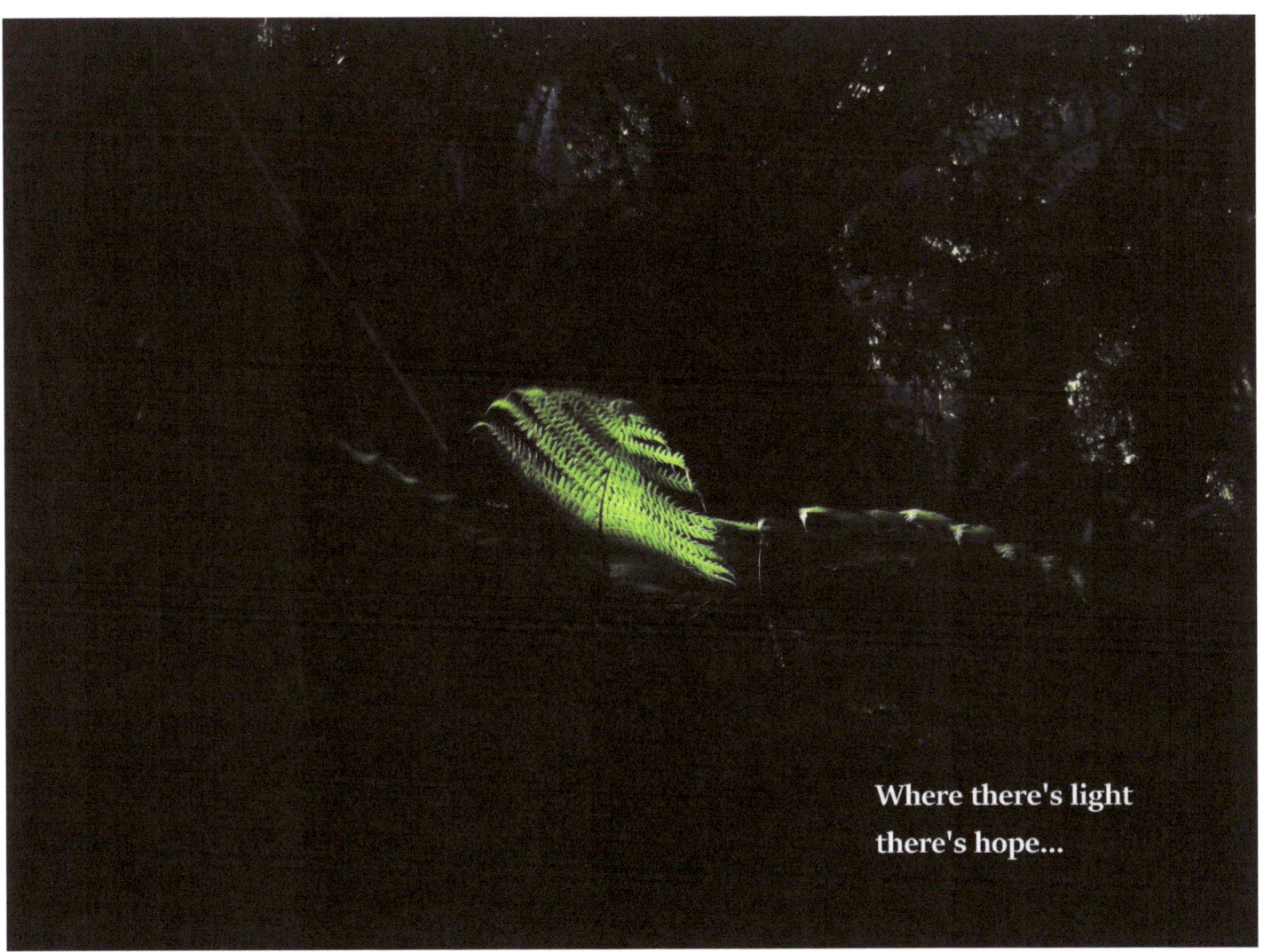

Where there's light
there's hope...

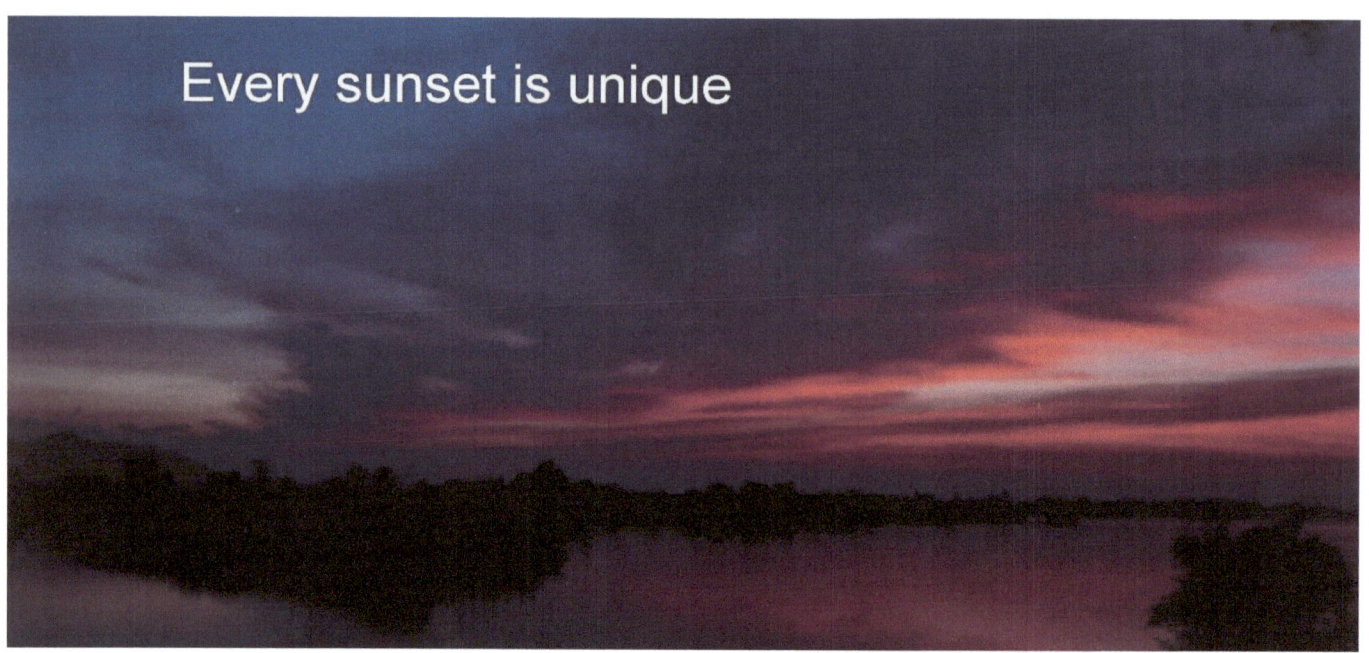

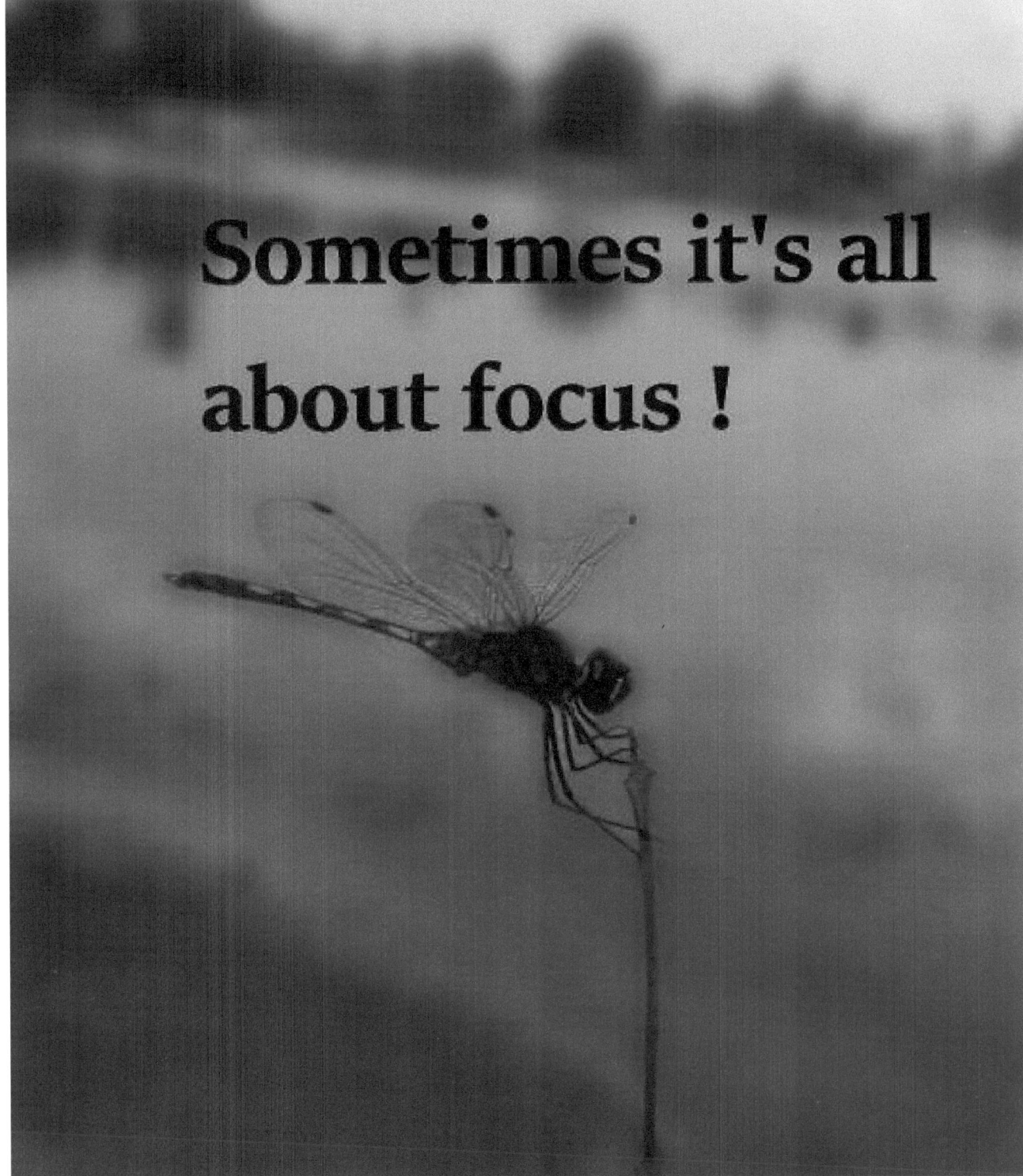

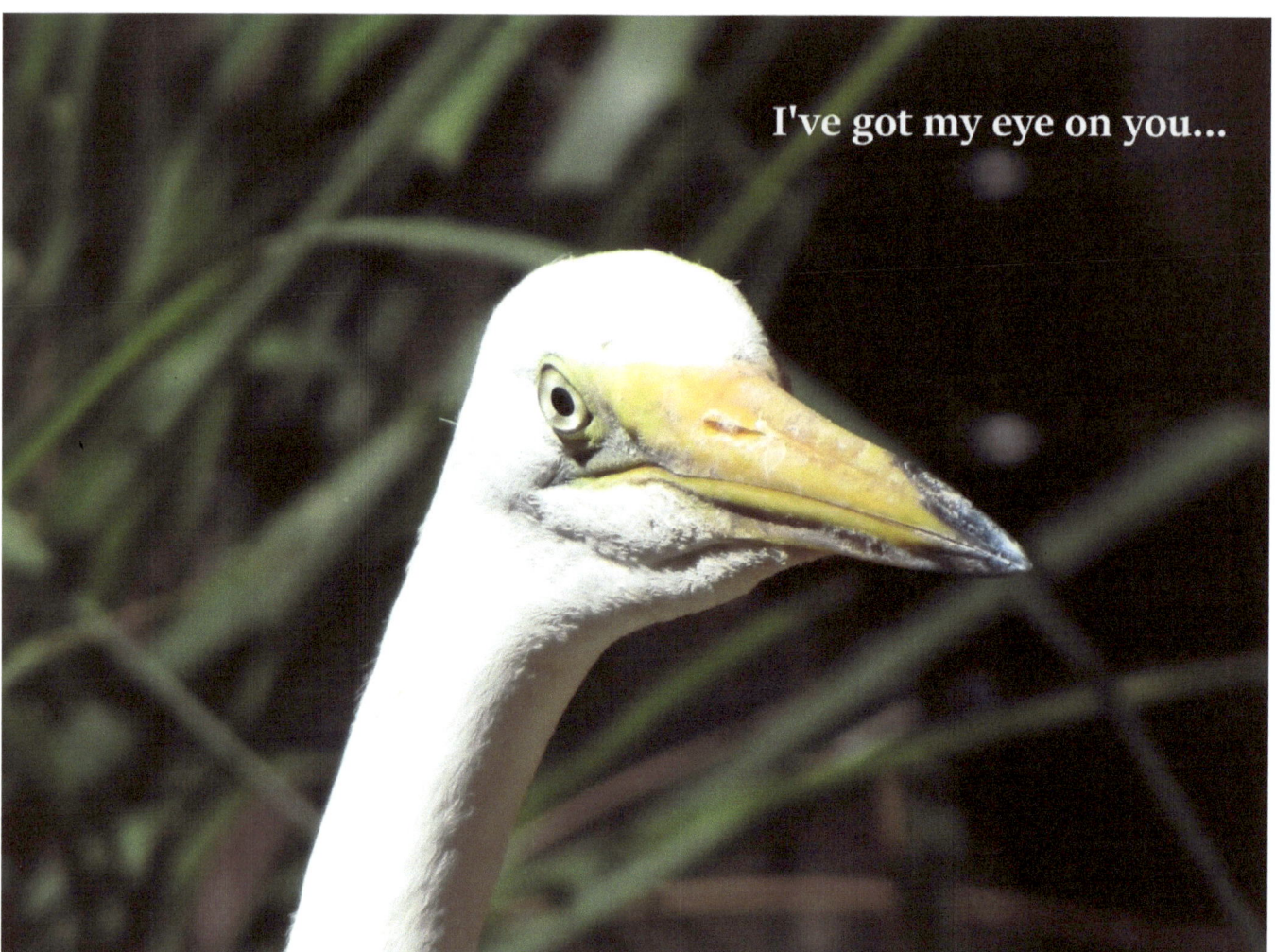

I've got my eye on you...

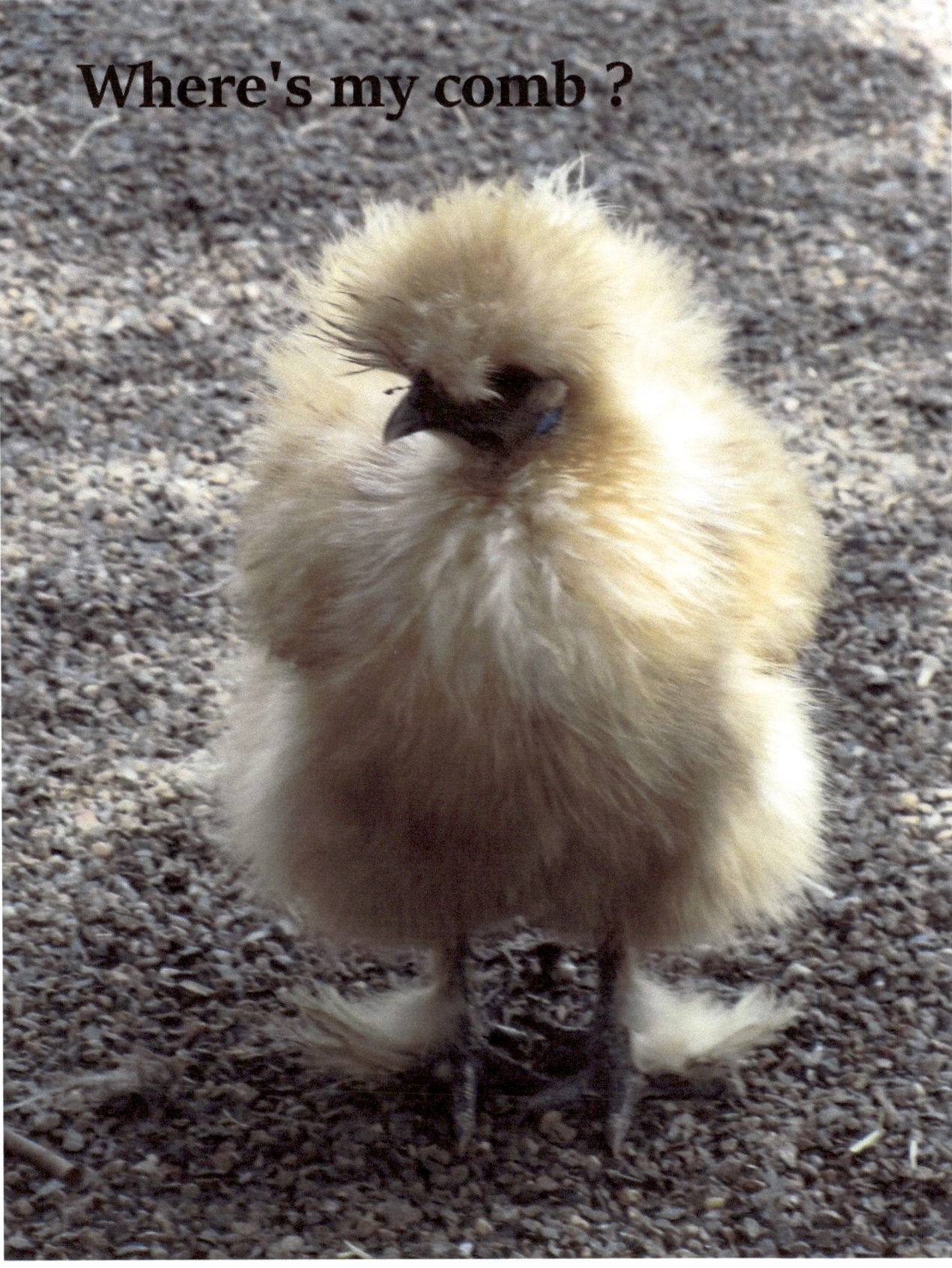

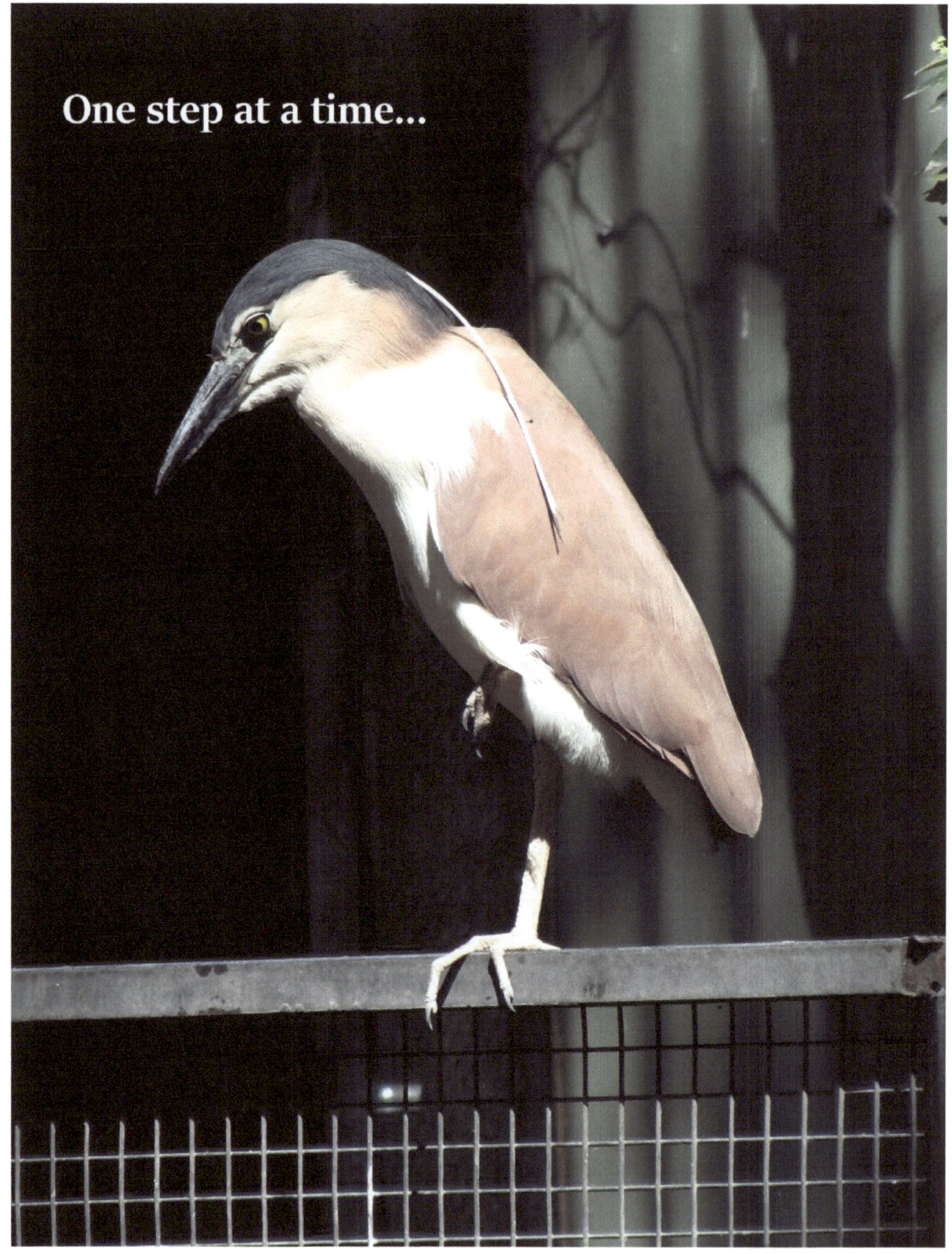

One step at a time...

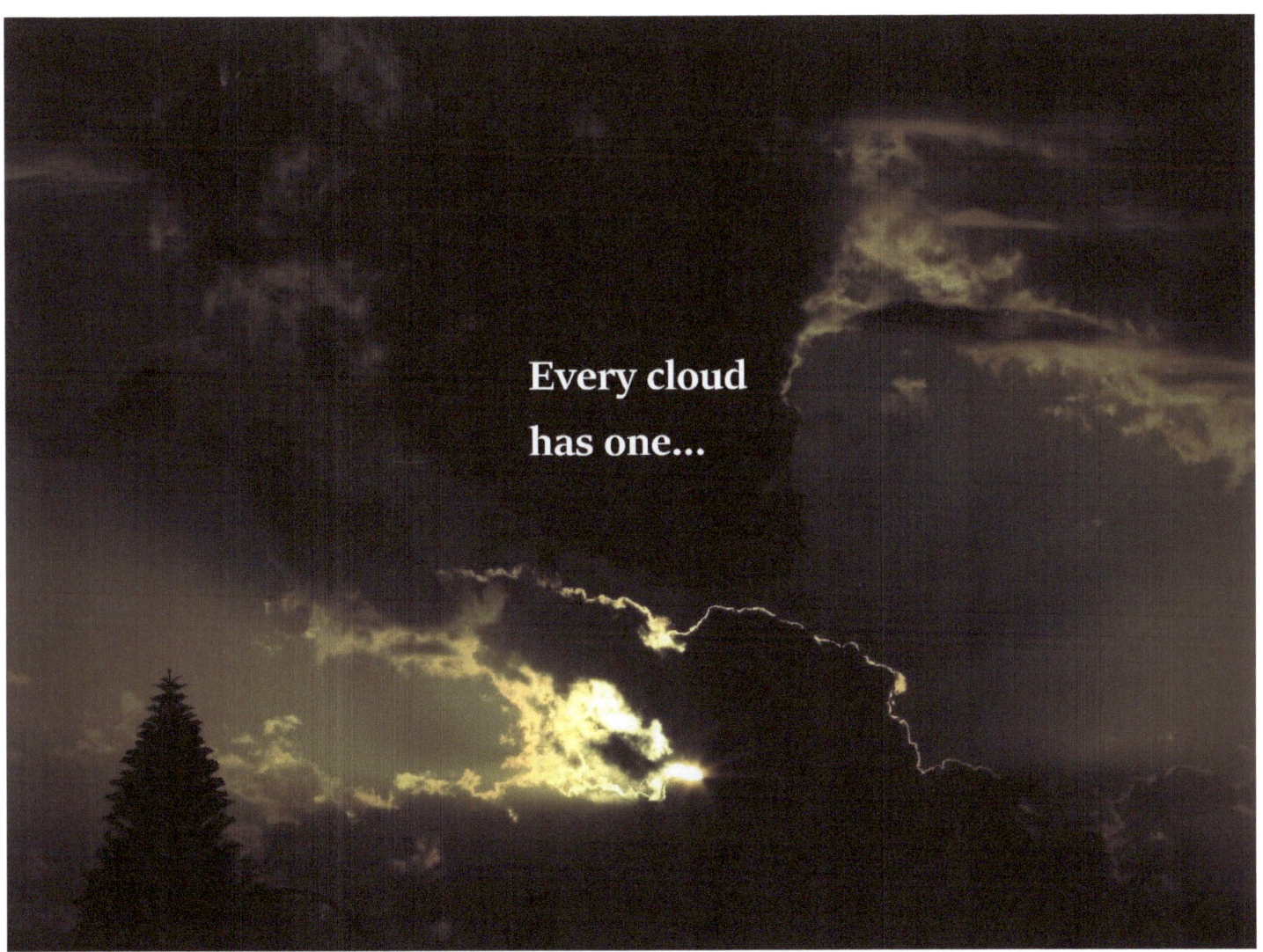

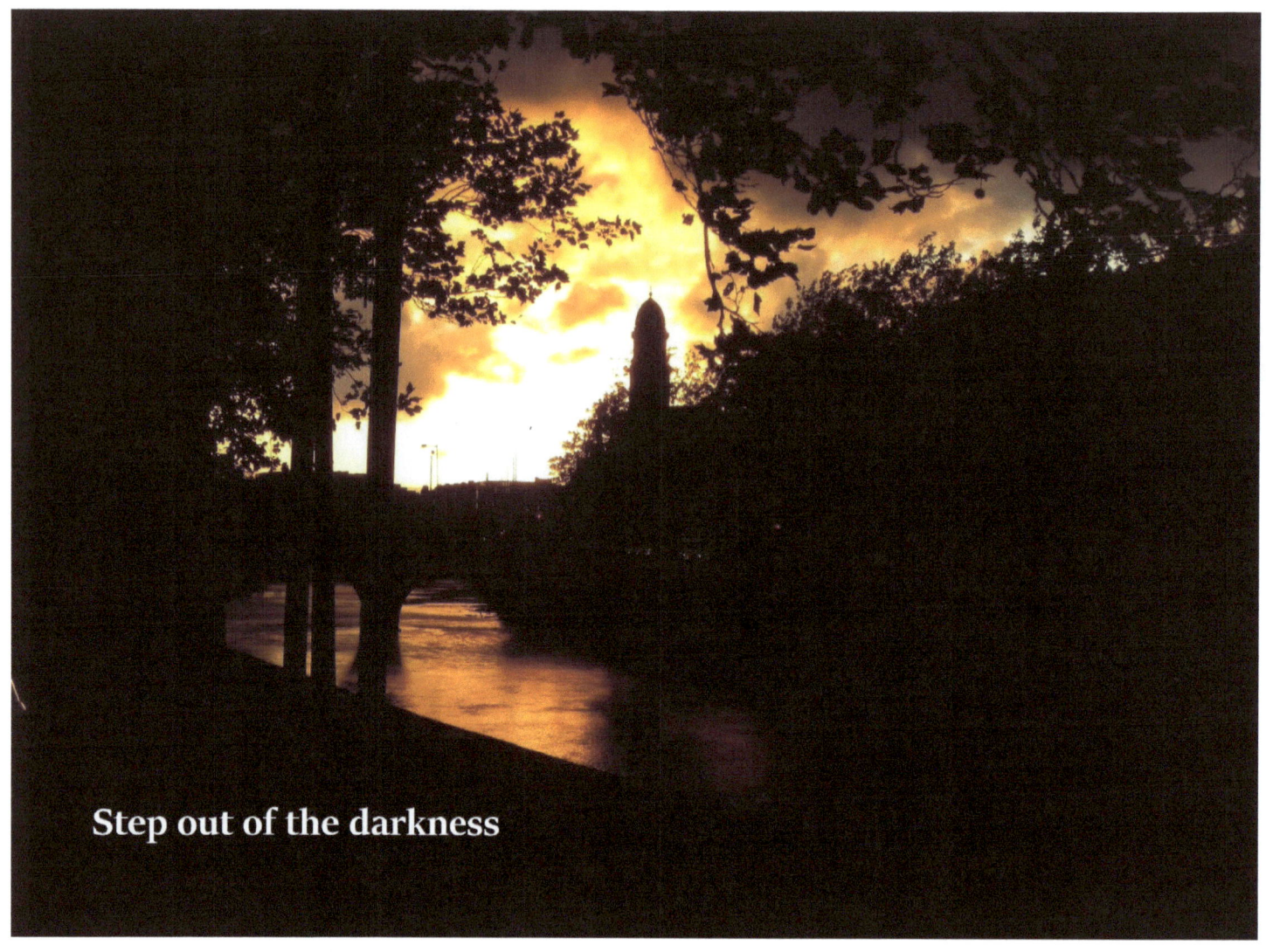

Step out of the darkness

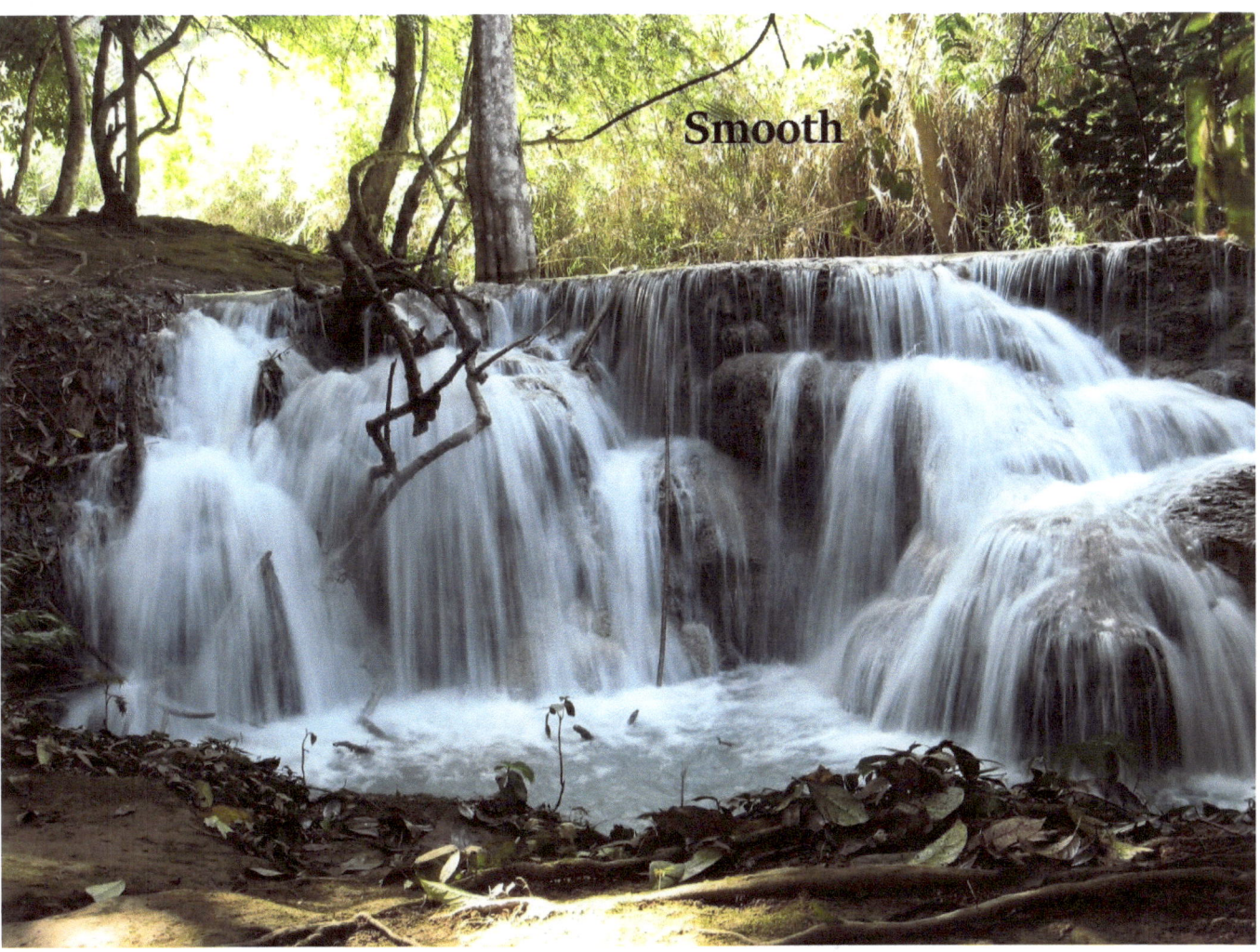

Never mind, the only way is up from here...

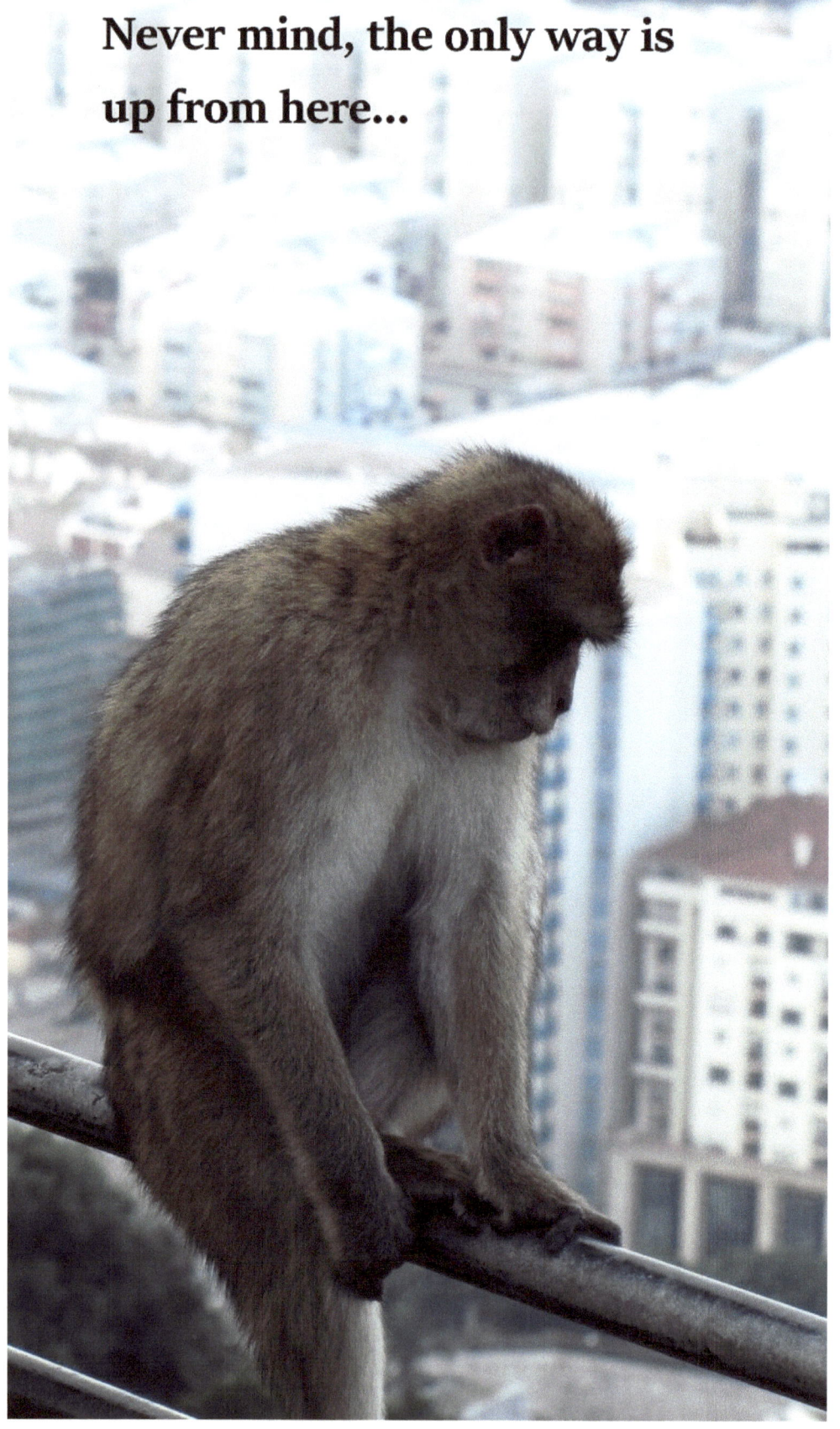

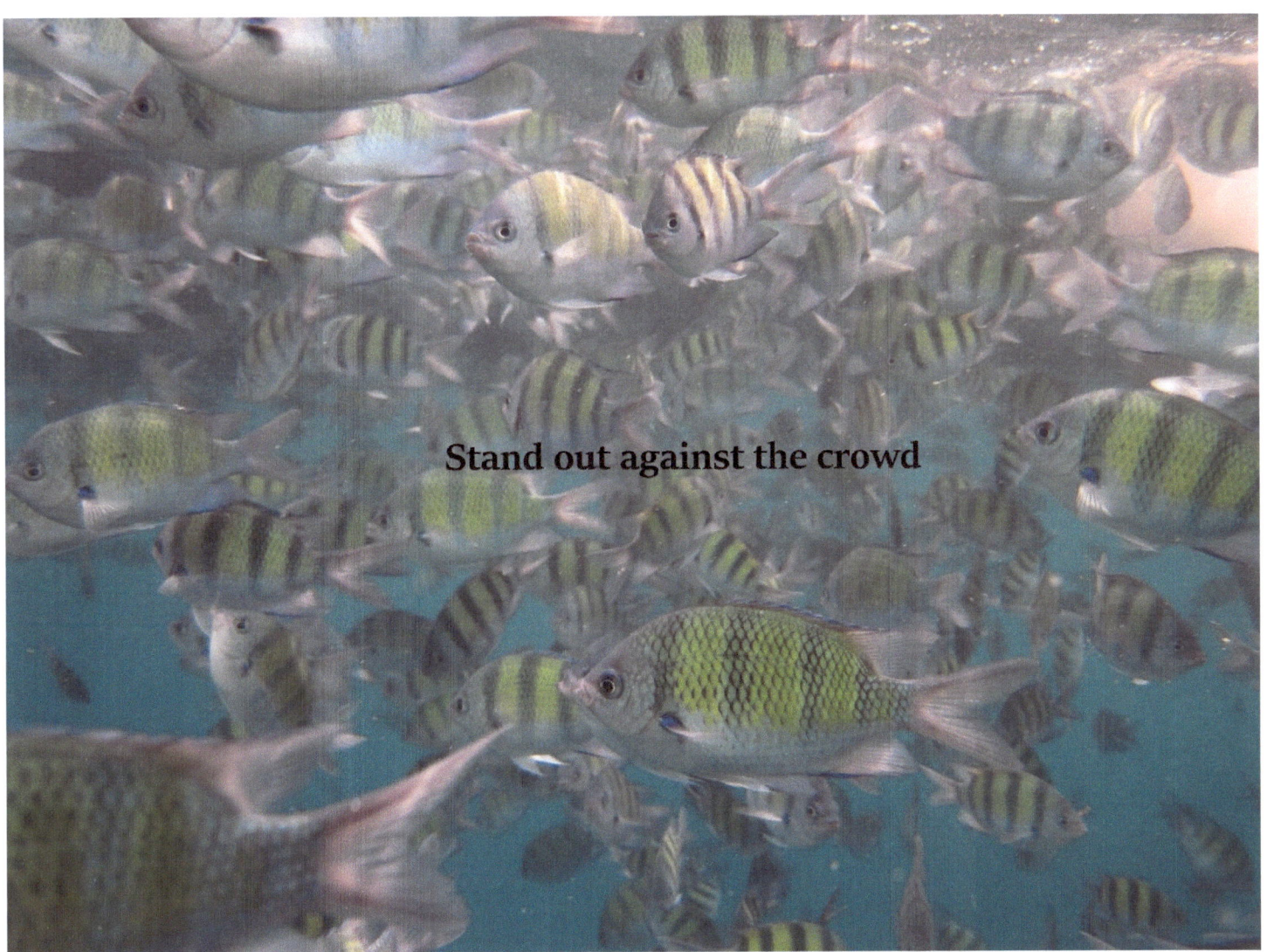

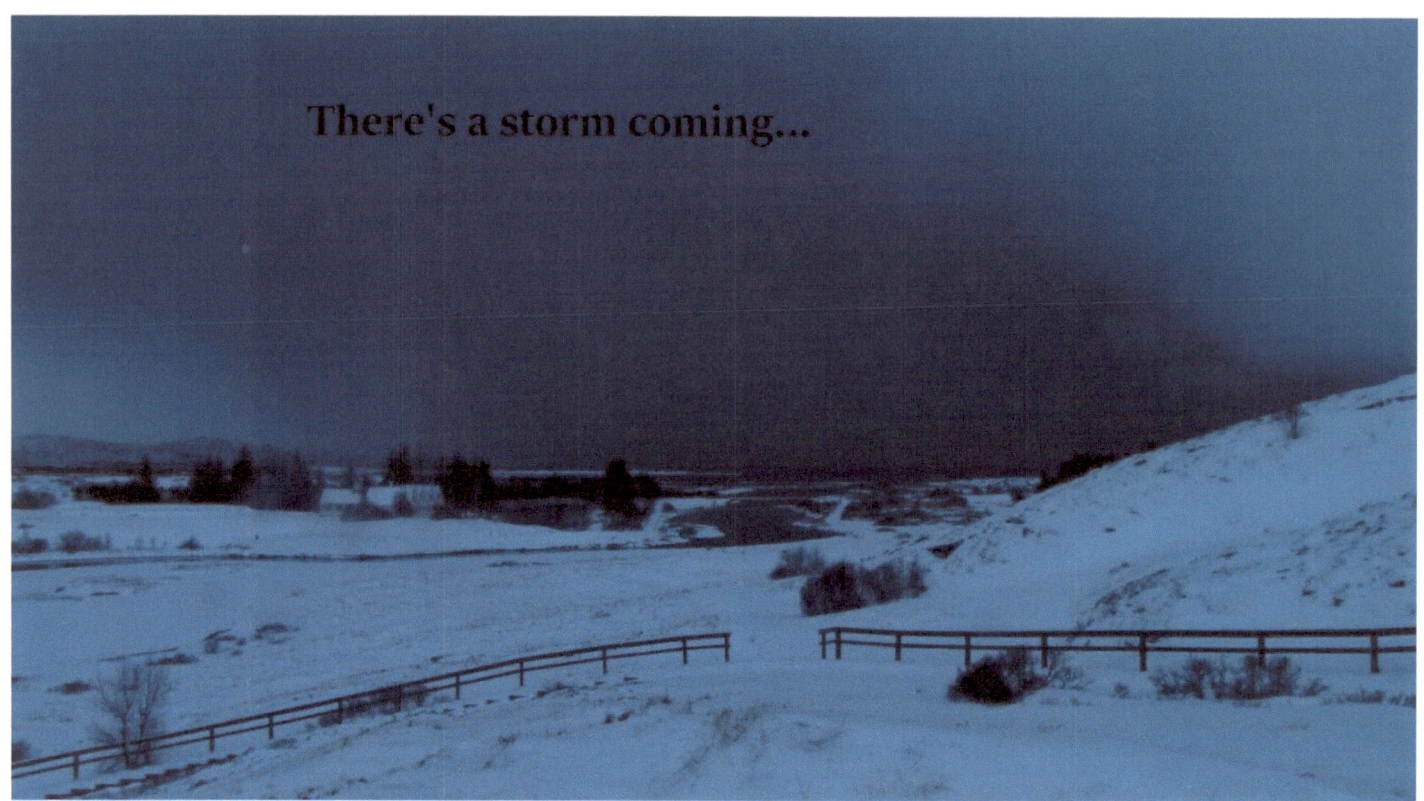

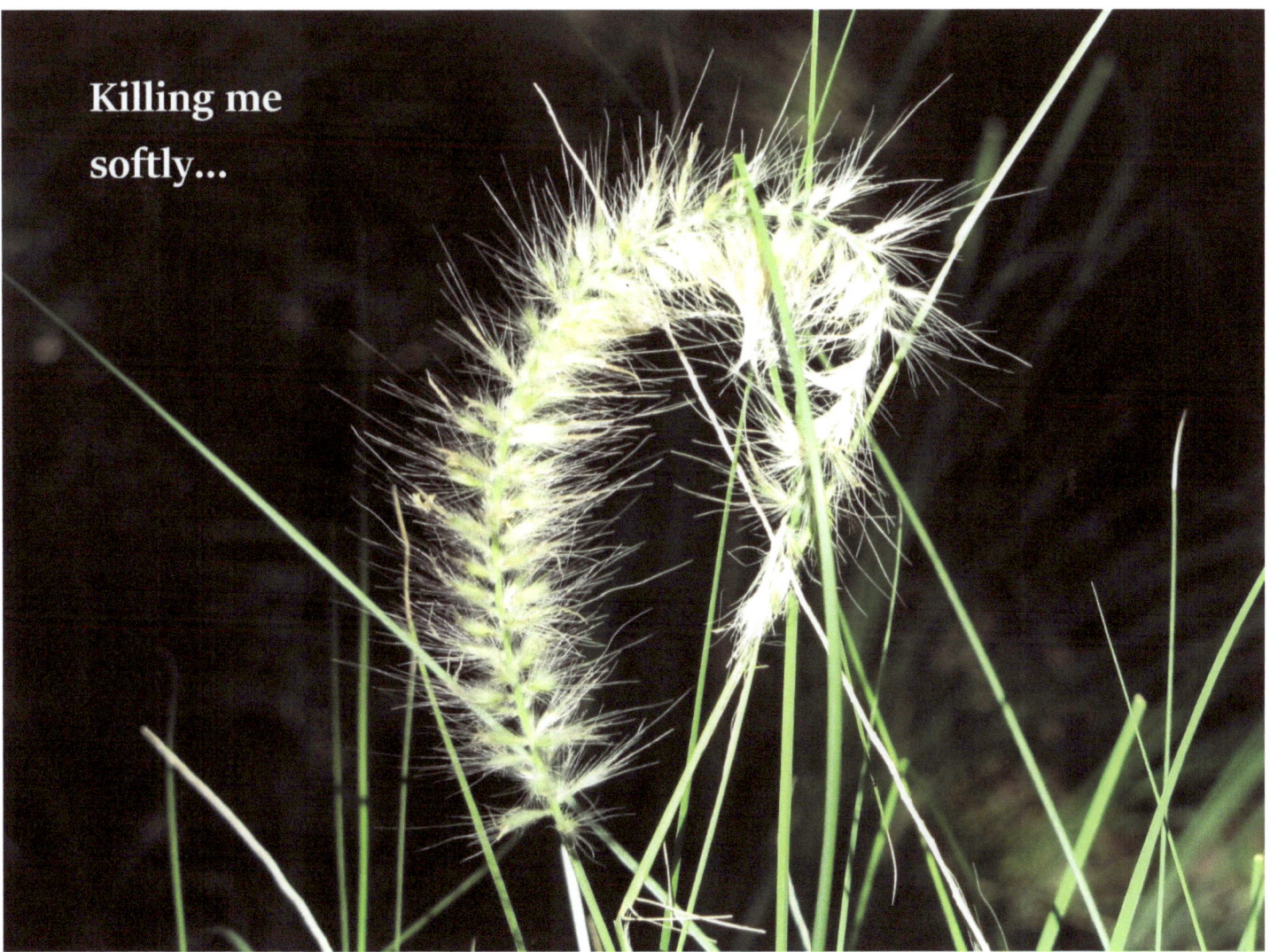

Killing me
softly...

Check the coast is clear
before venturing out

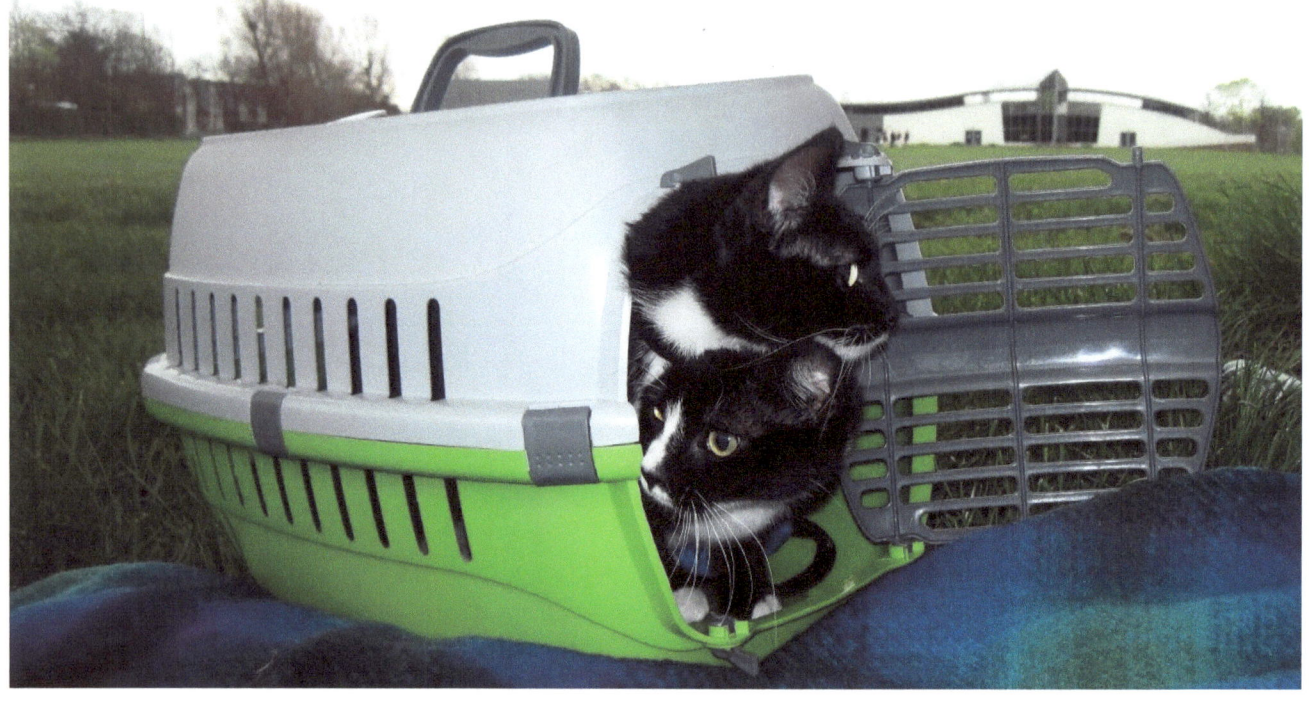

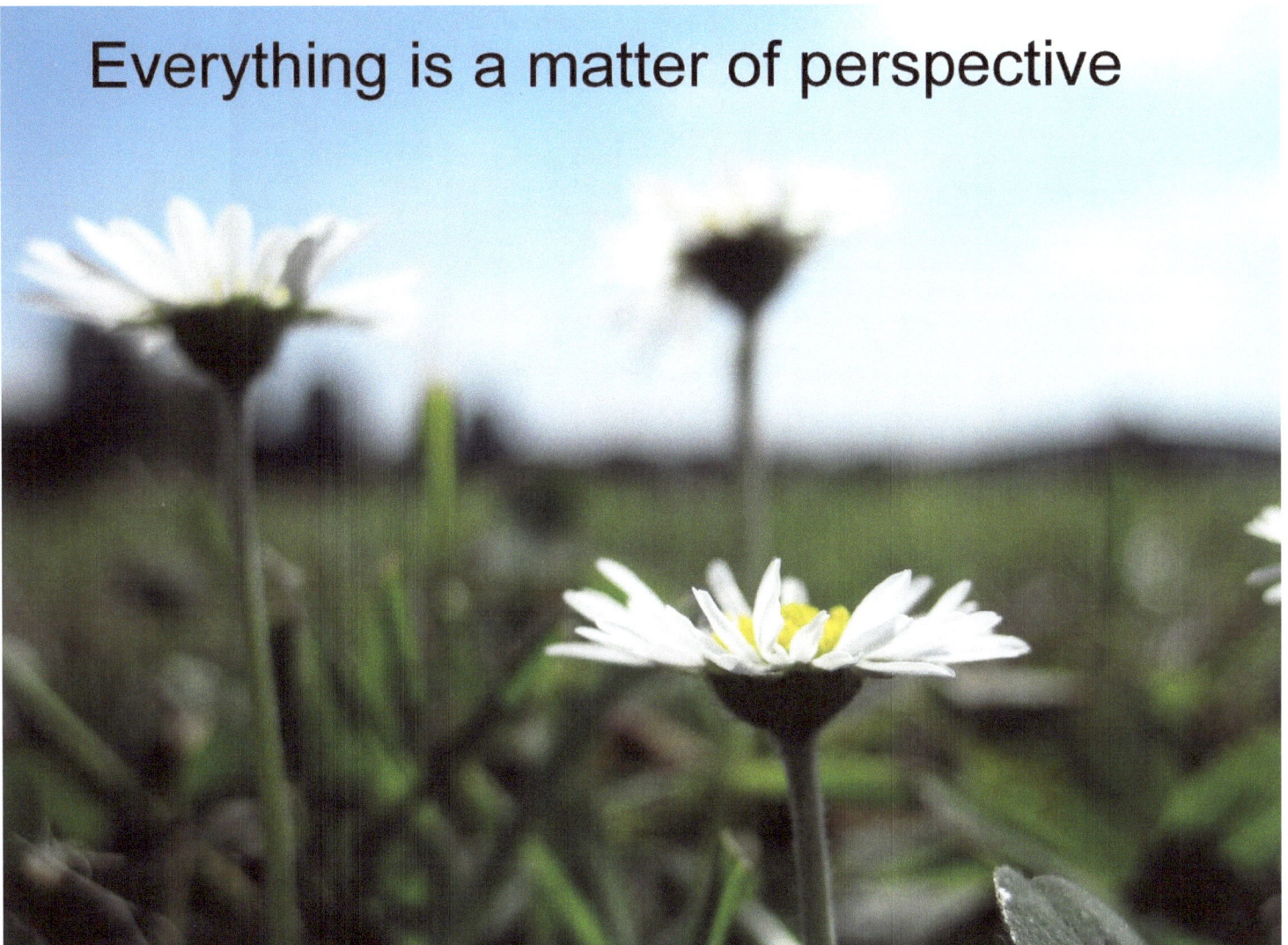

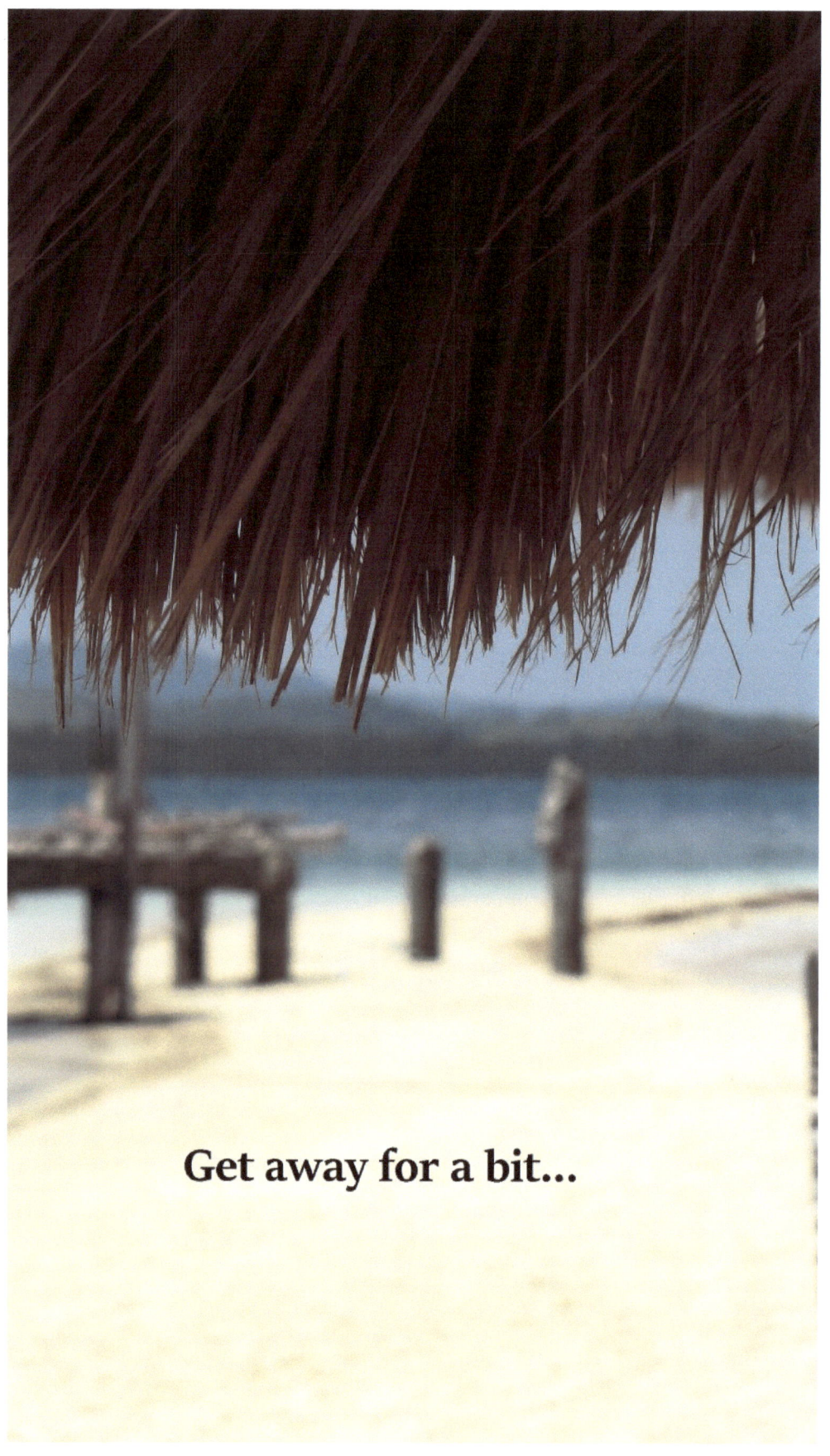

Get away for a bit...

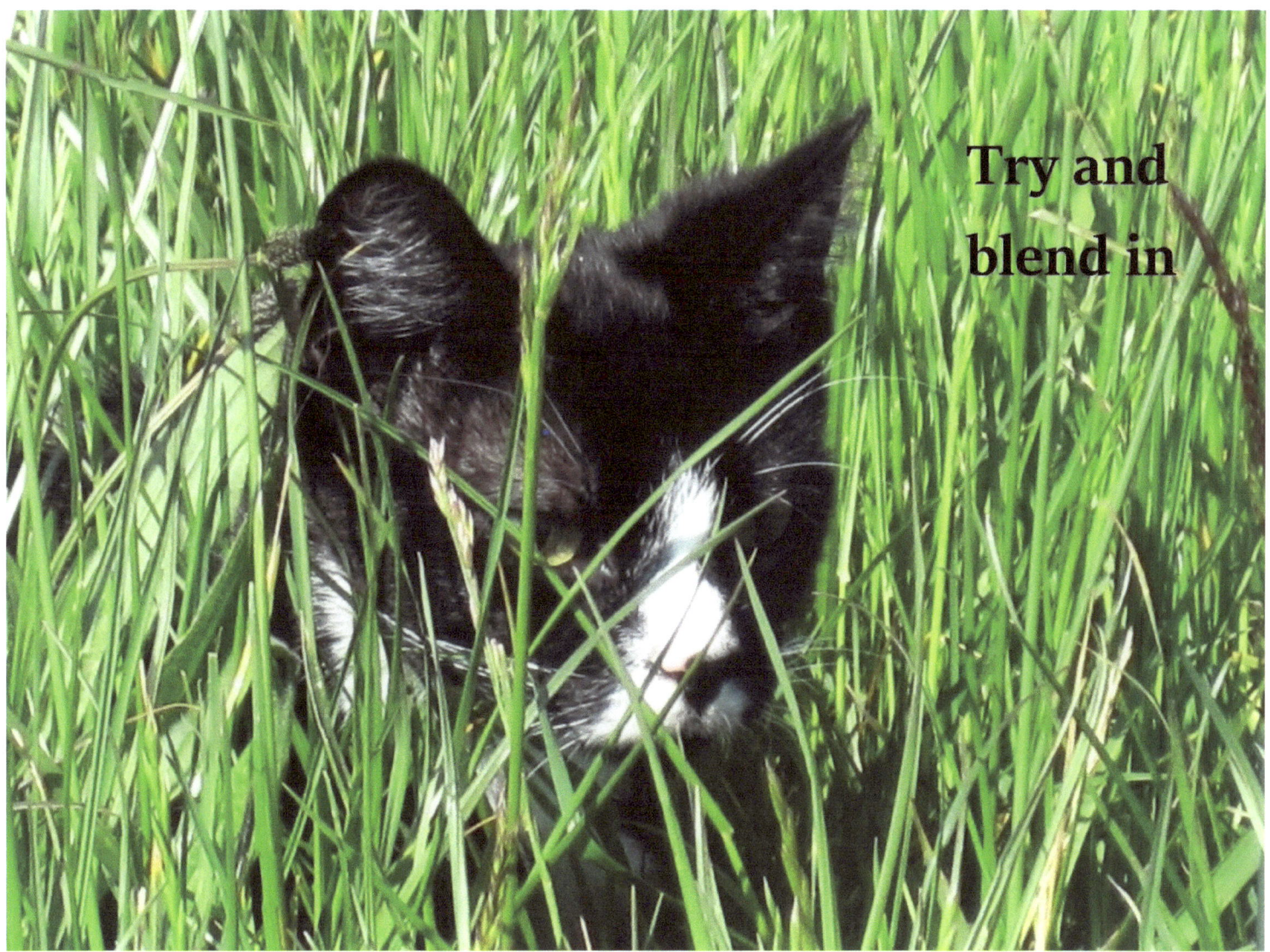

**Try and
blend in**

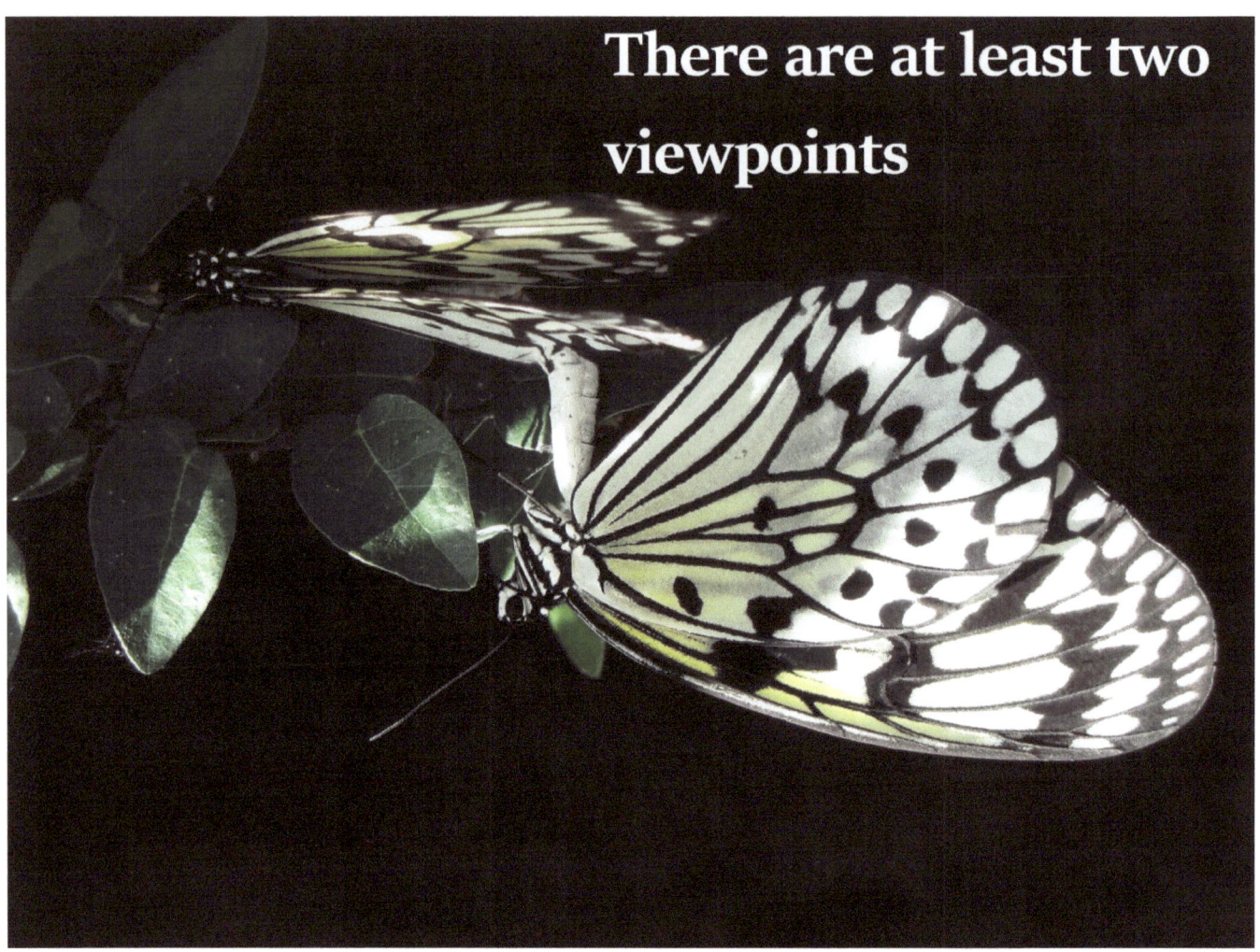

There are at least two viewpoints

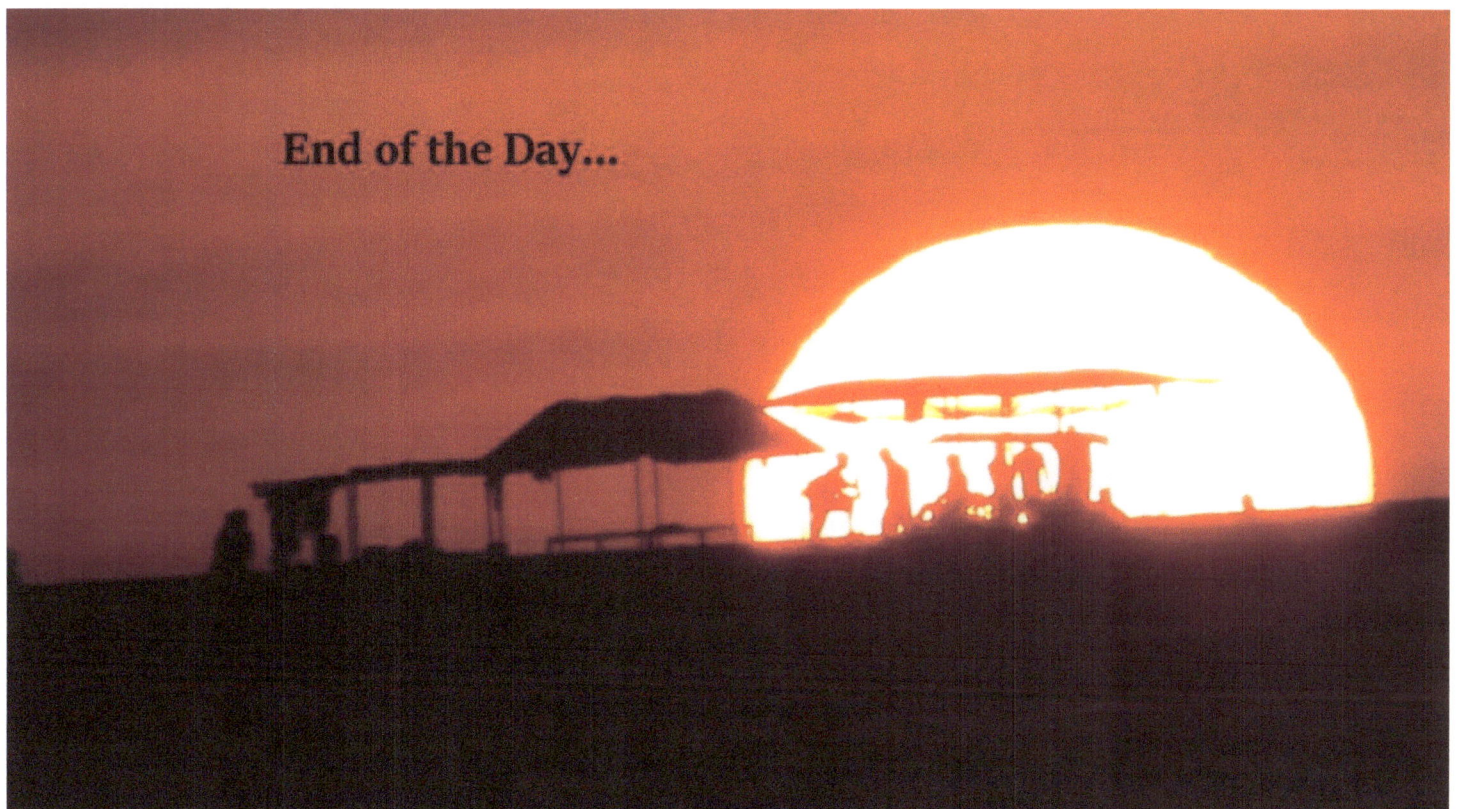

End of the Day...

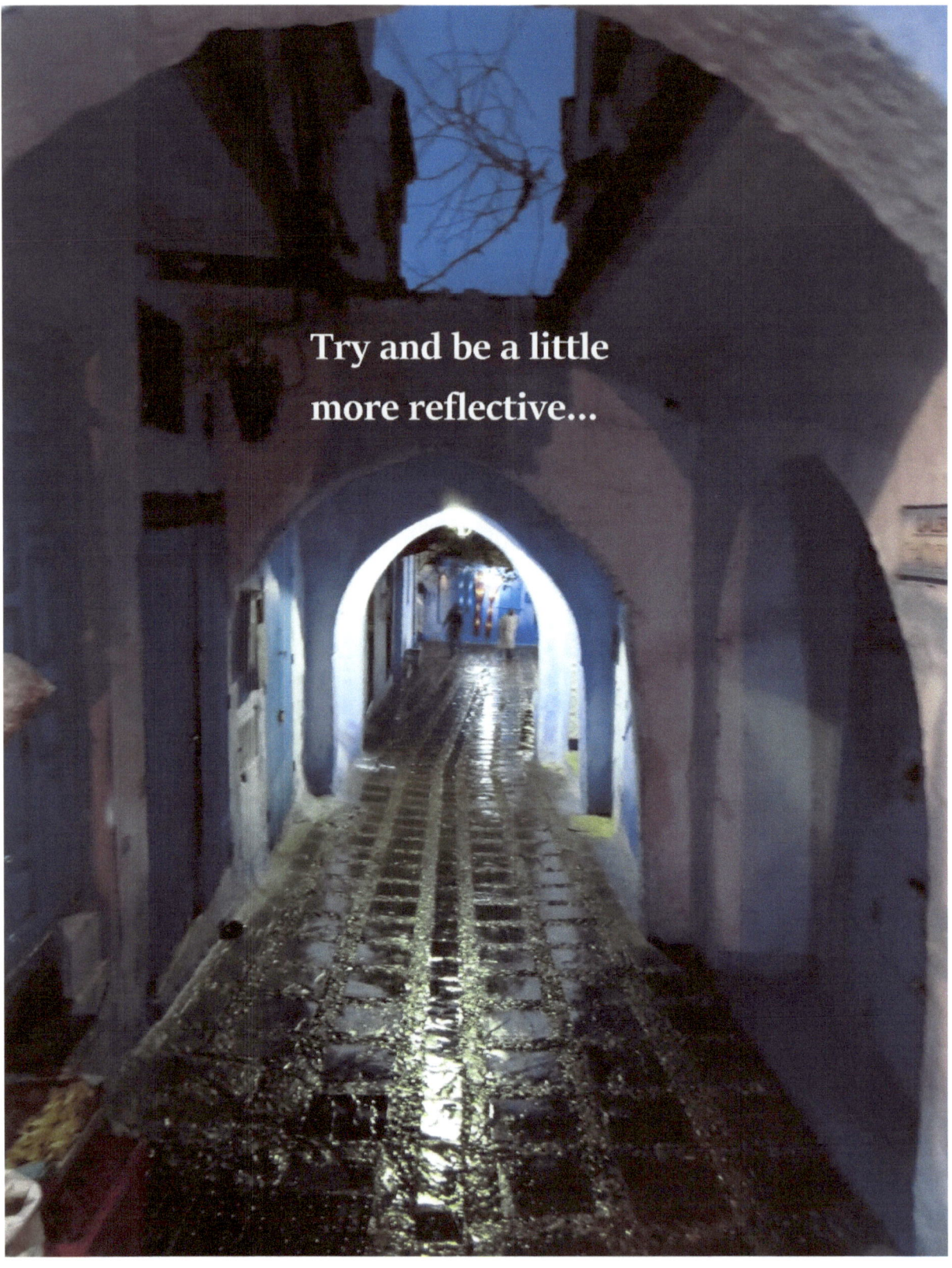

Try and be a little
more reflective...

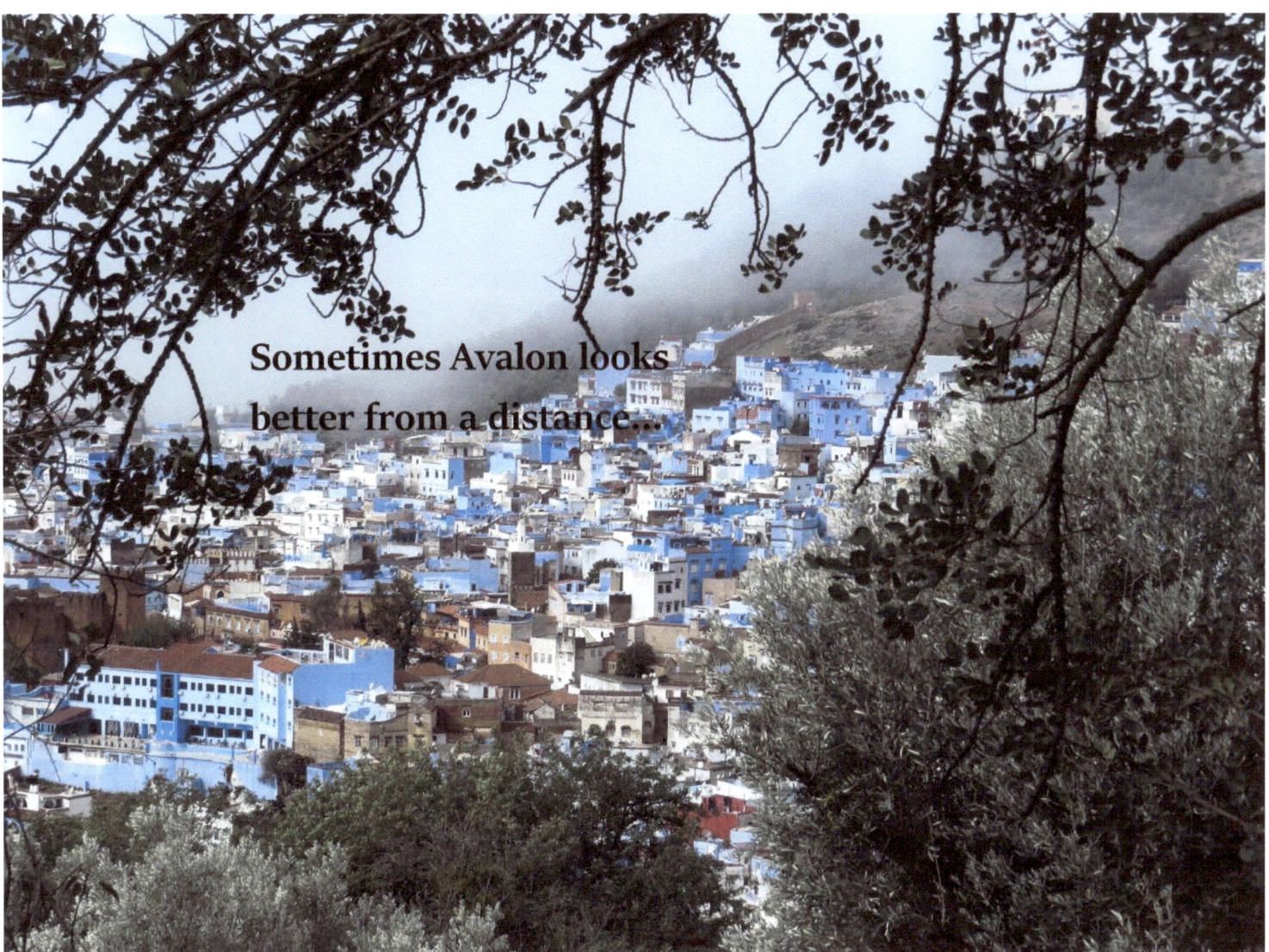

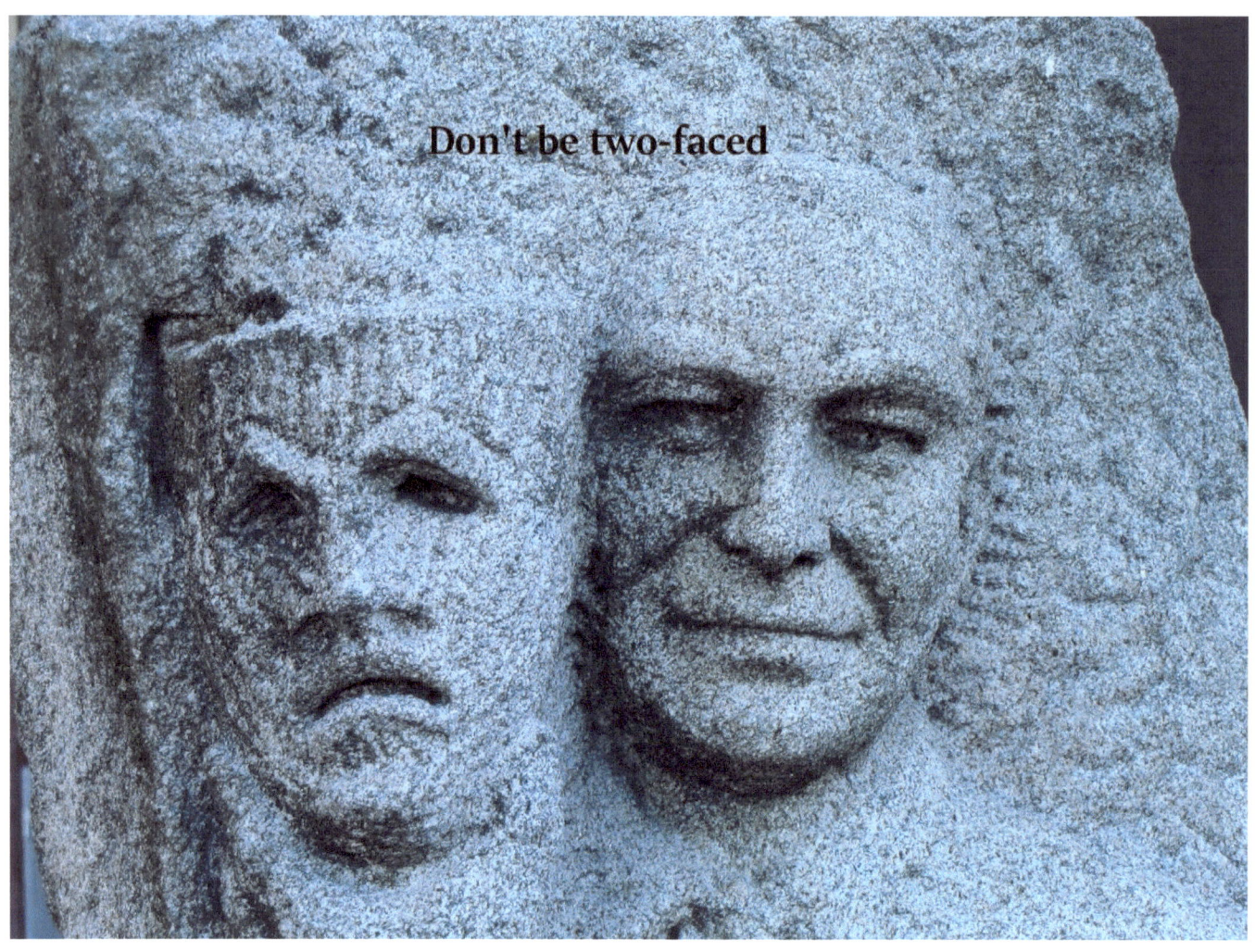

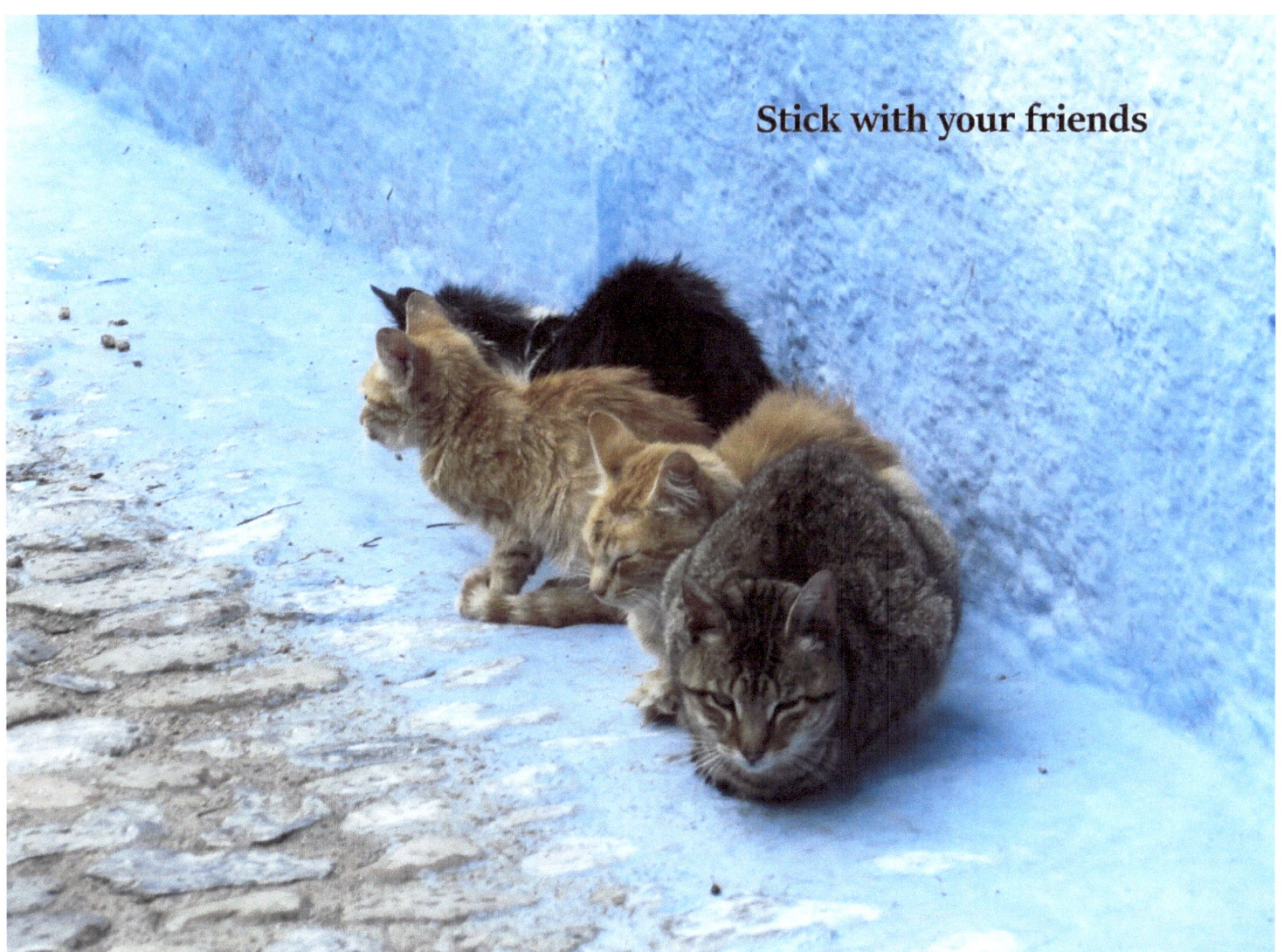

Stick with your friends

David Leahy

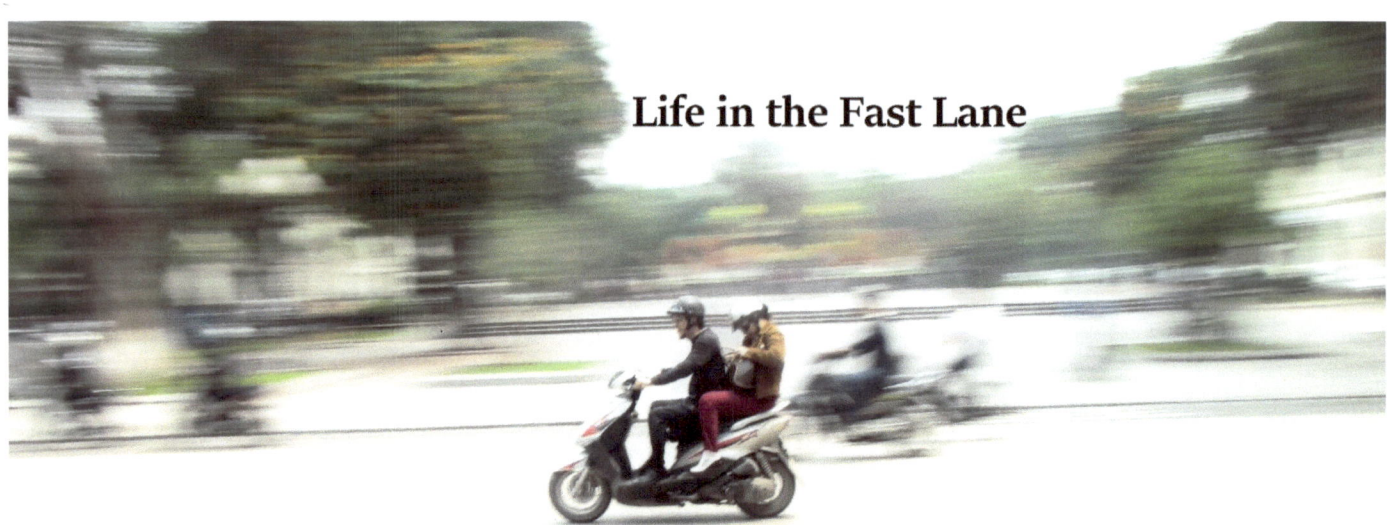

Life in the Fast Lane

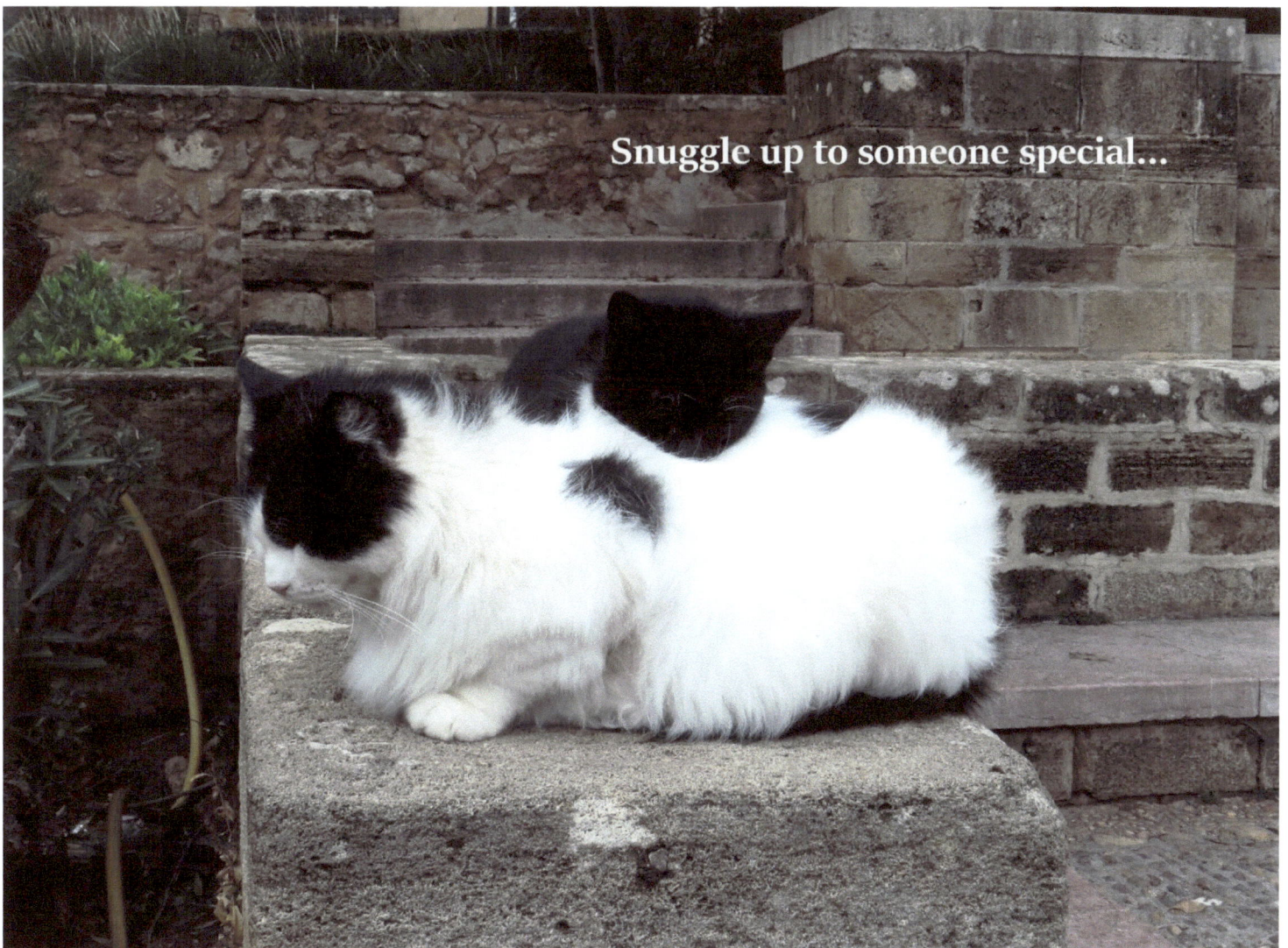

Snuggle up to someone special...

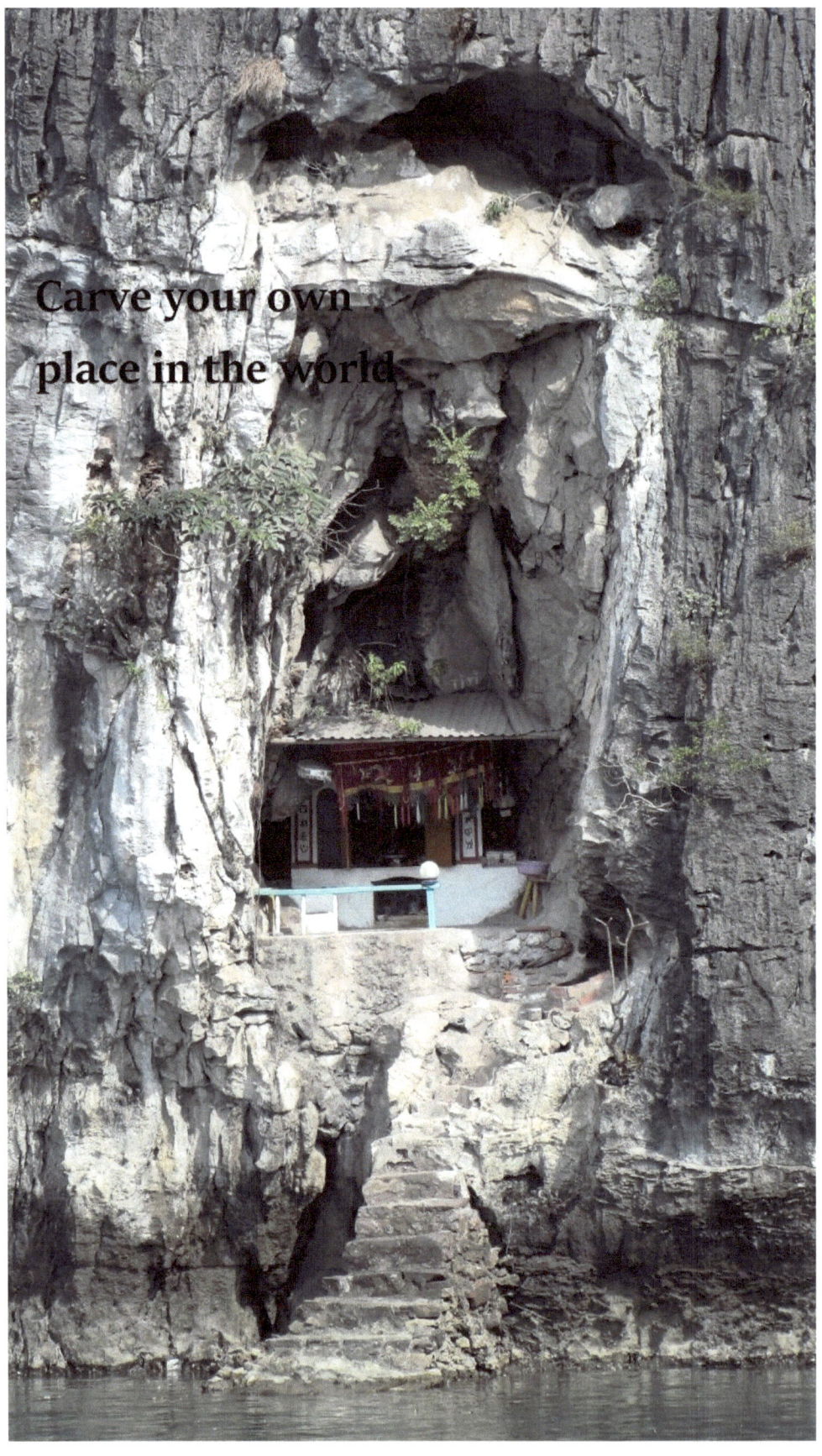

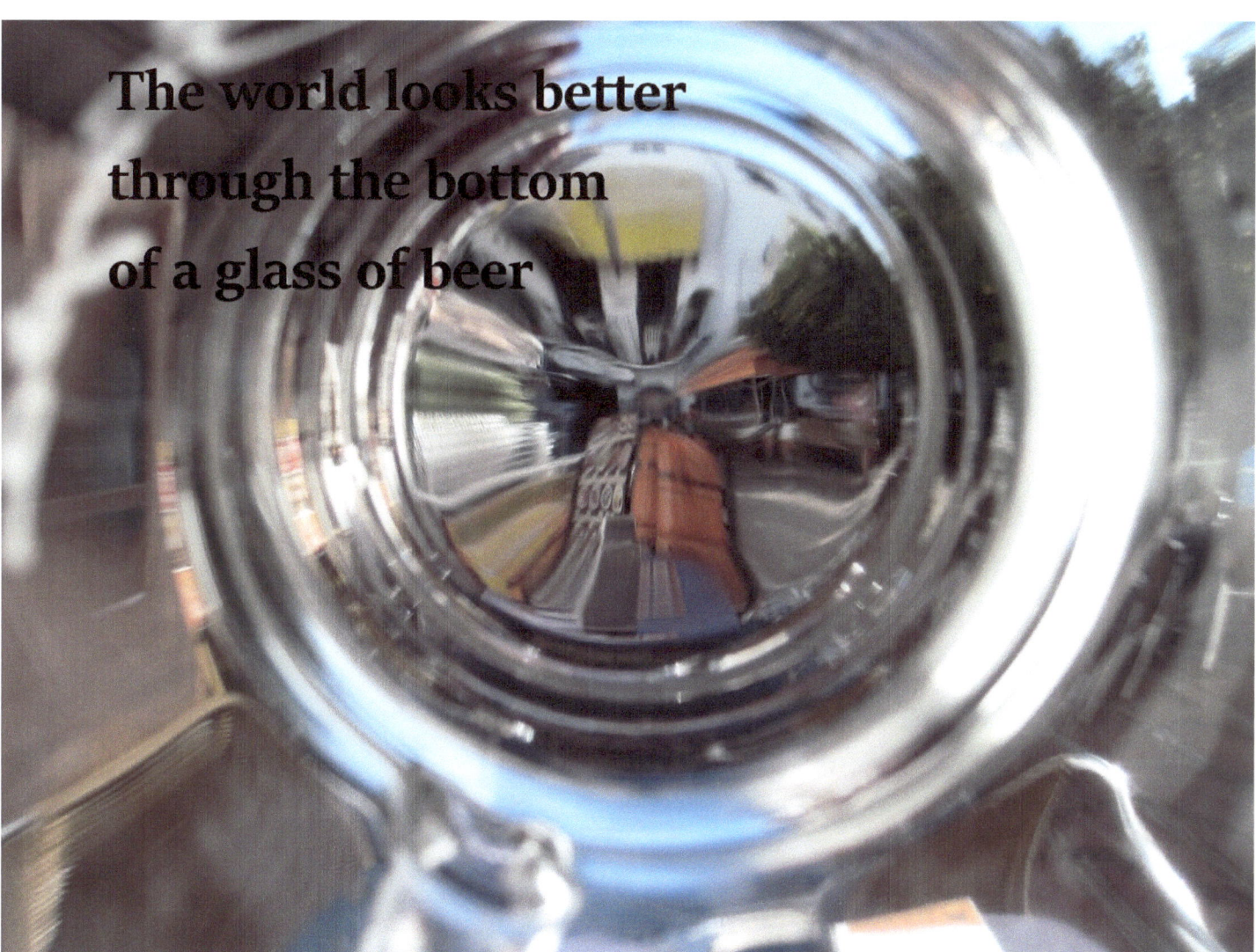

The world looks better through the bottom of a glass of beer

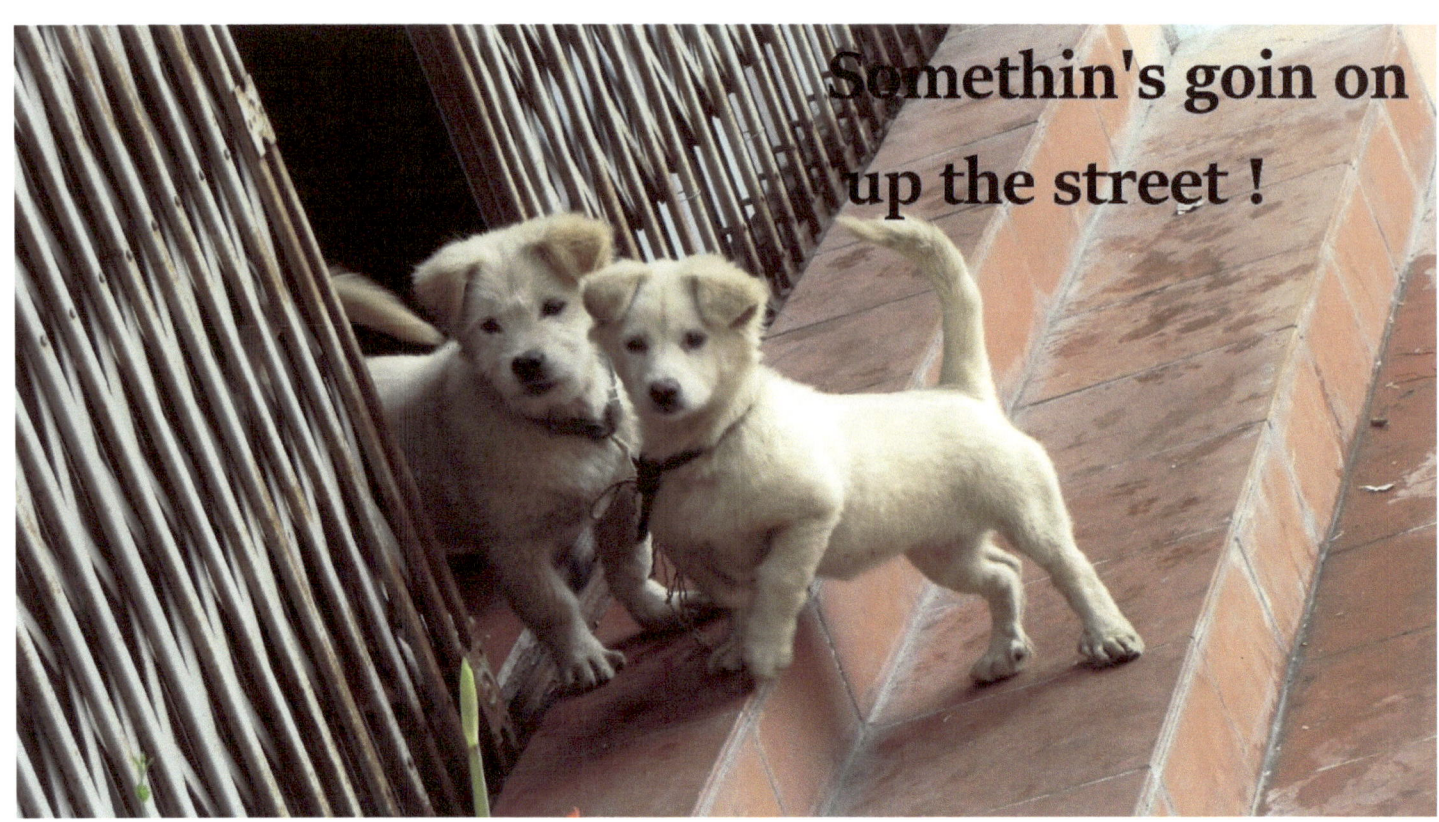

Somethin's goin on up the street !

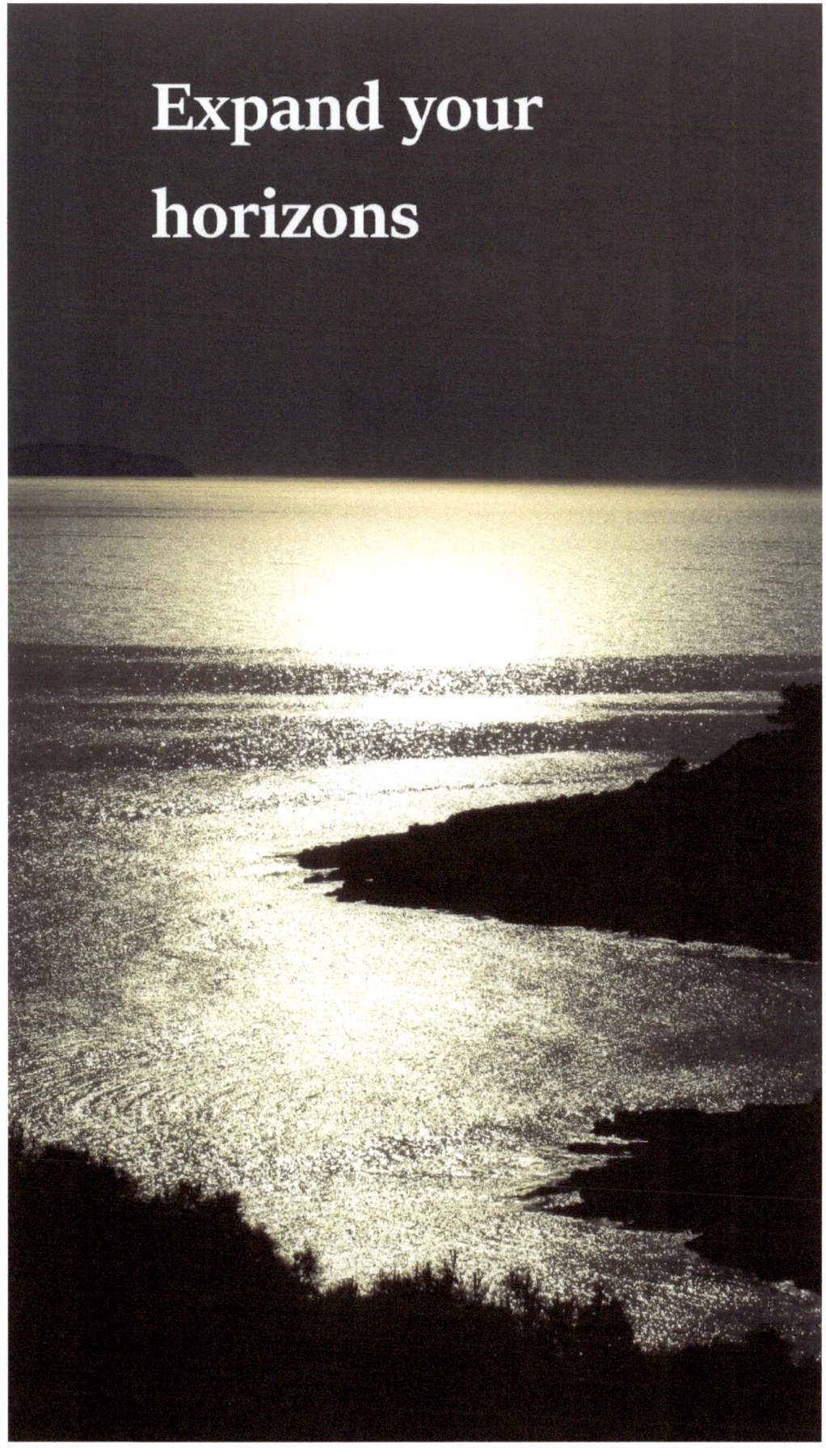

Expand your horizons

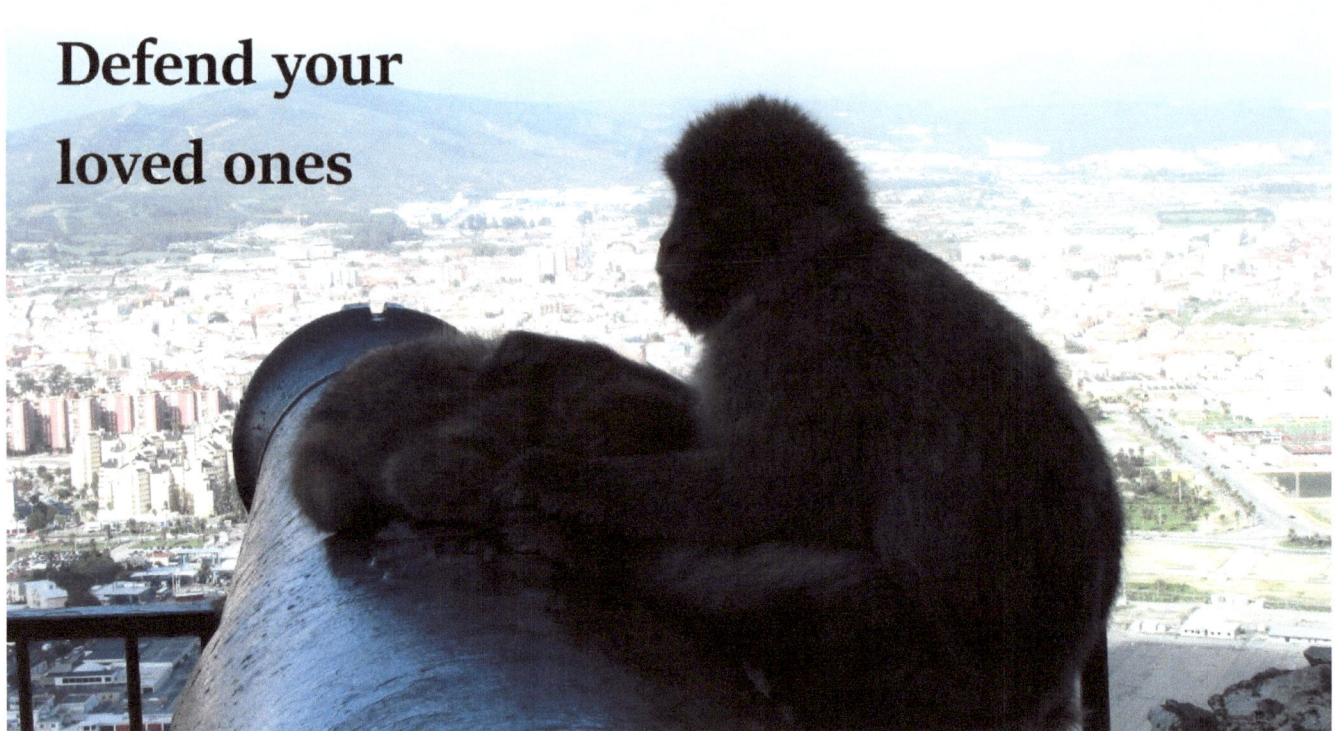

**Defend your
loved ones**

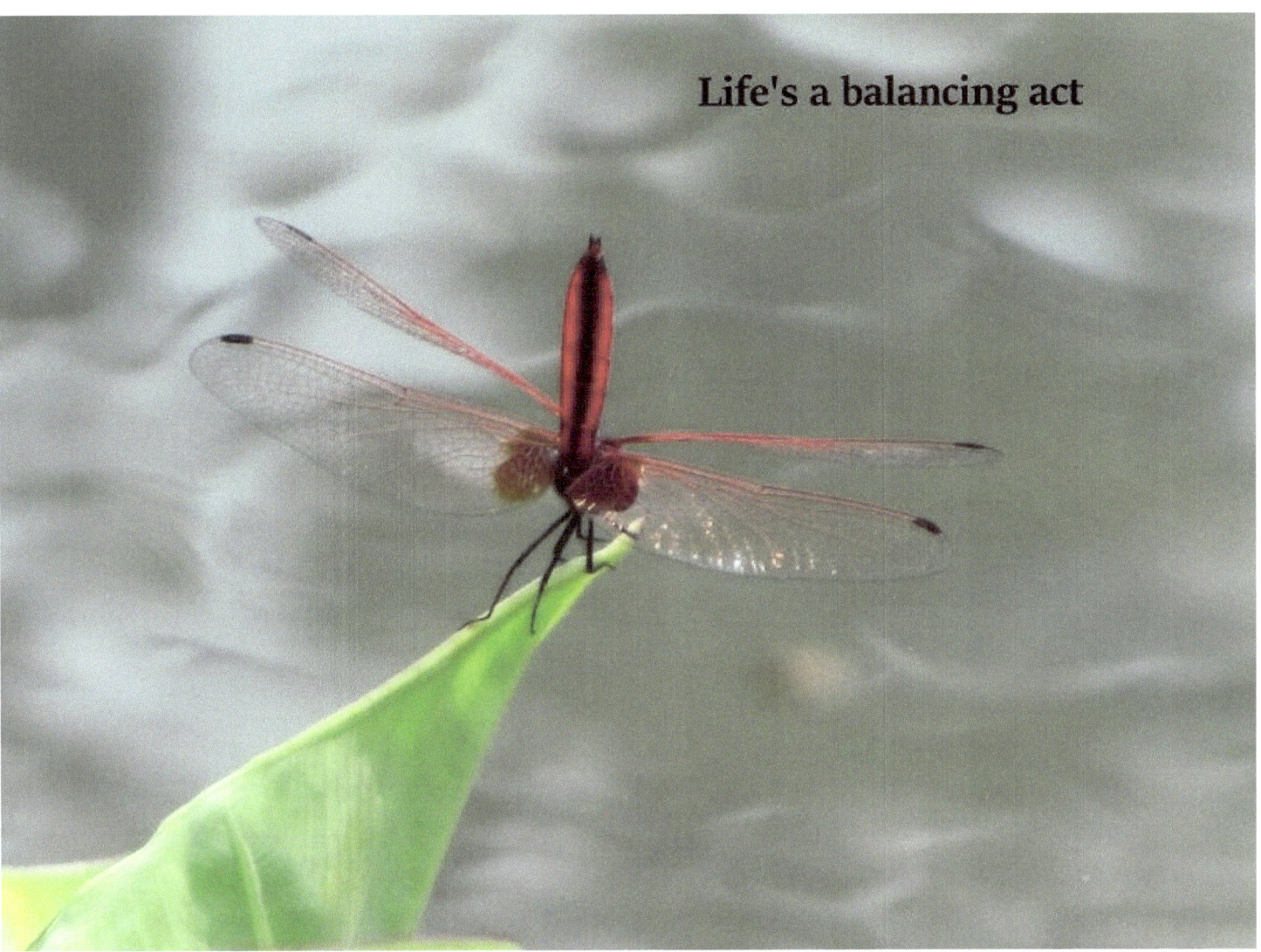

Life's a balancing act

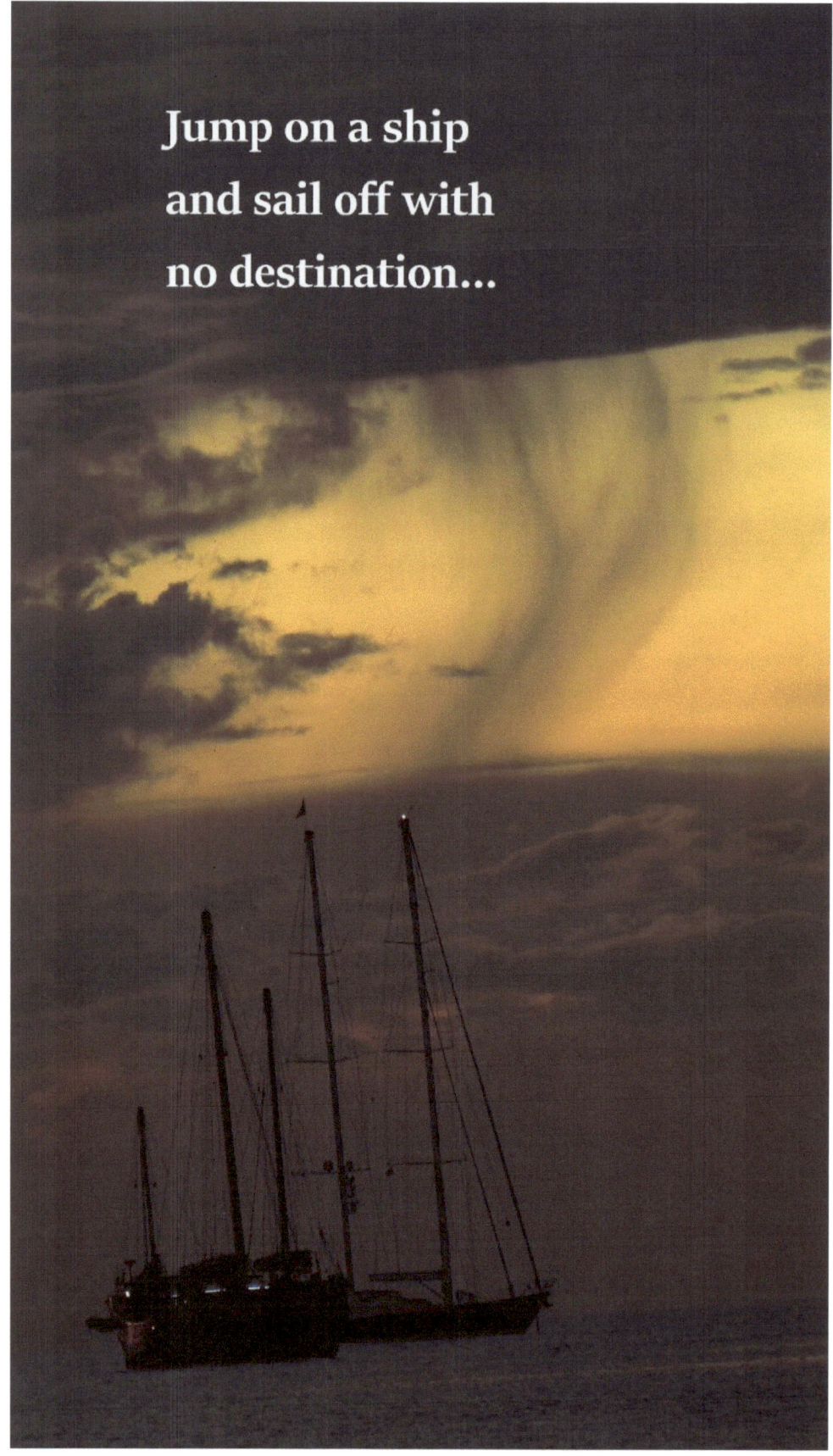

Jump on a ship
and sail off with
no destination...

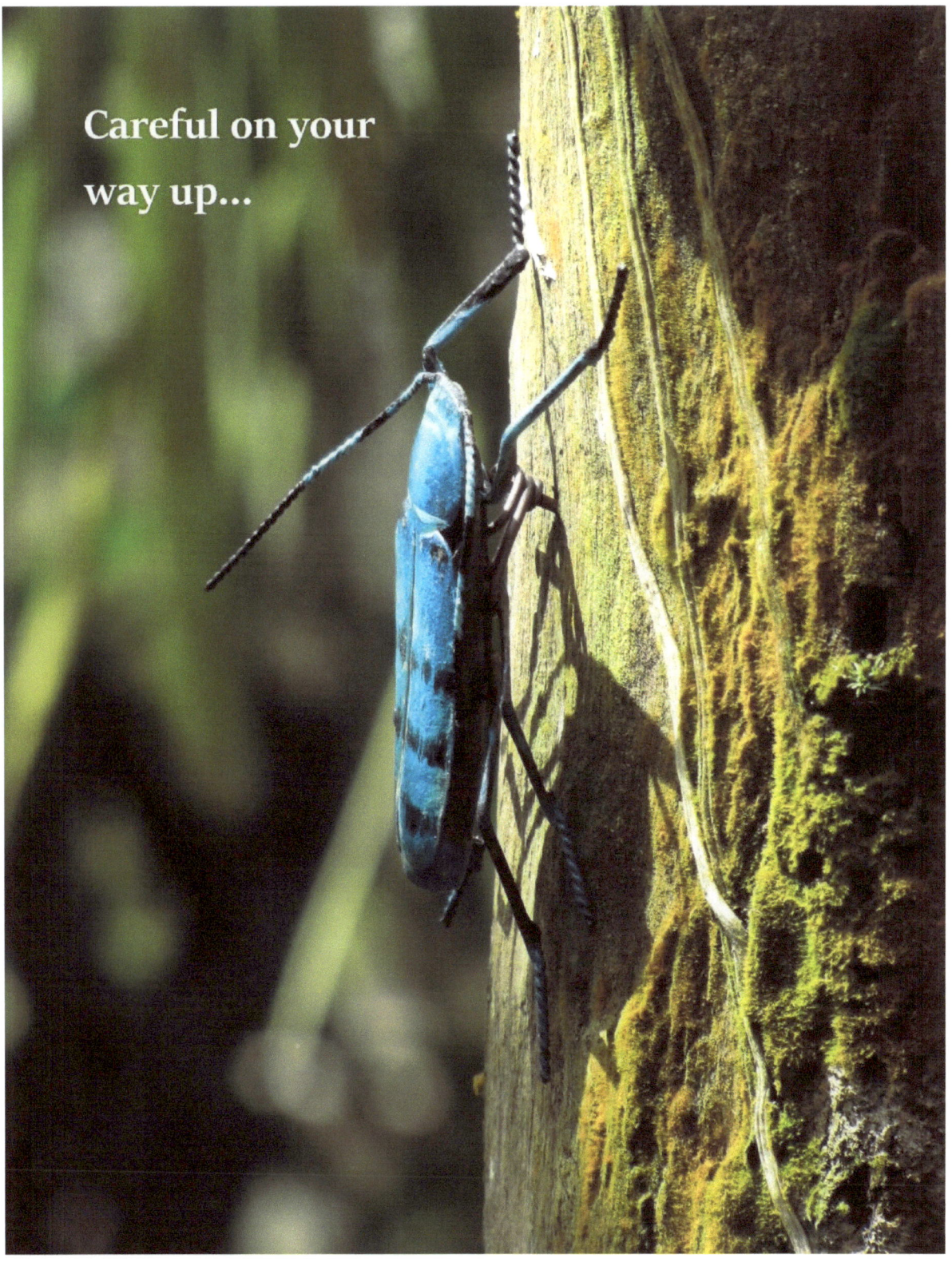

Careful on your way up...

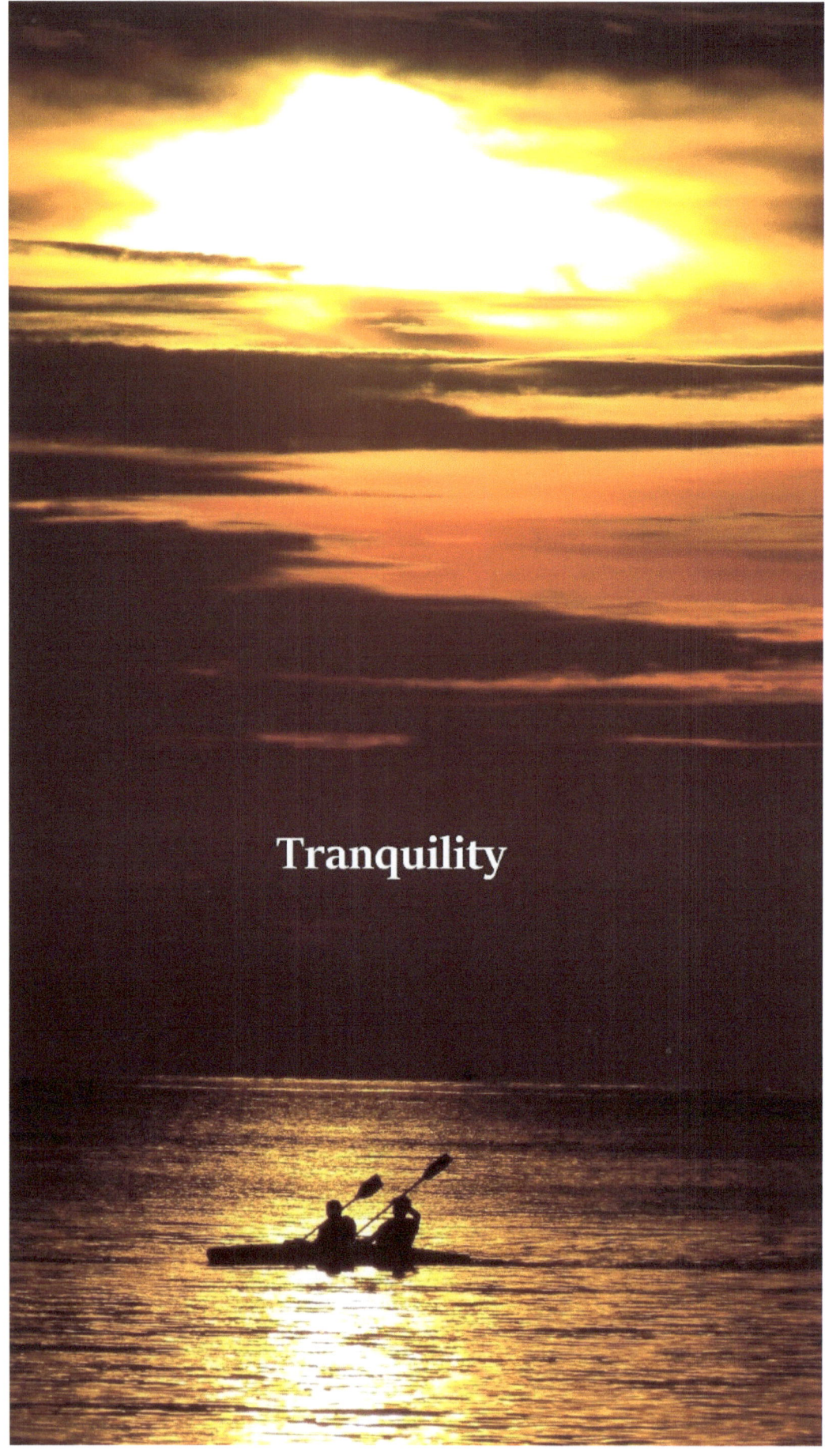

Tranquility

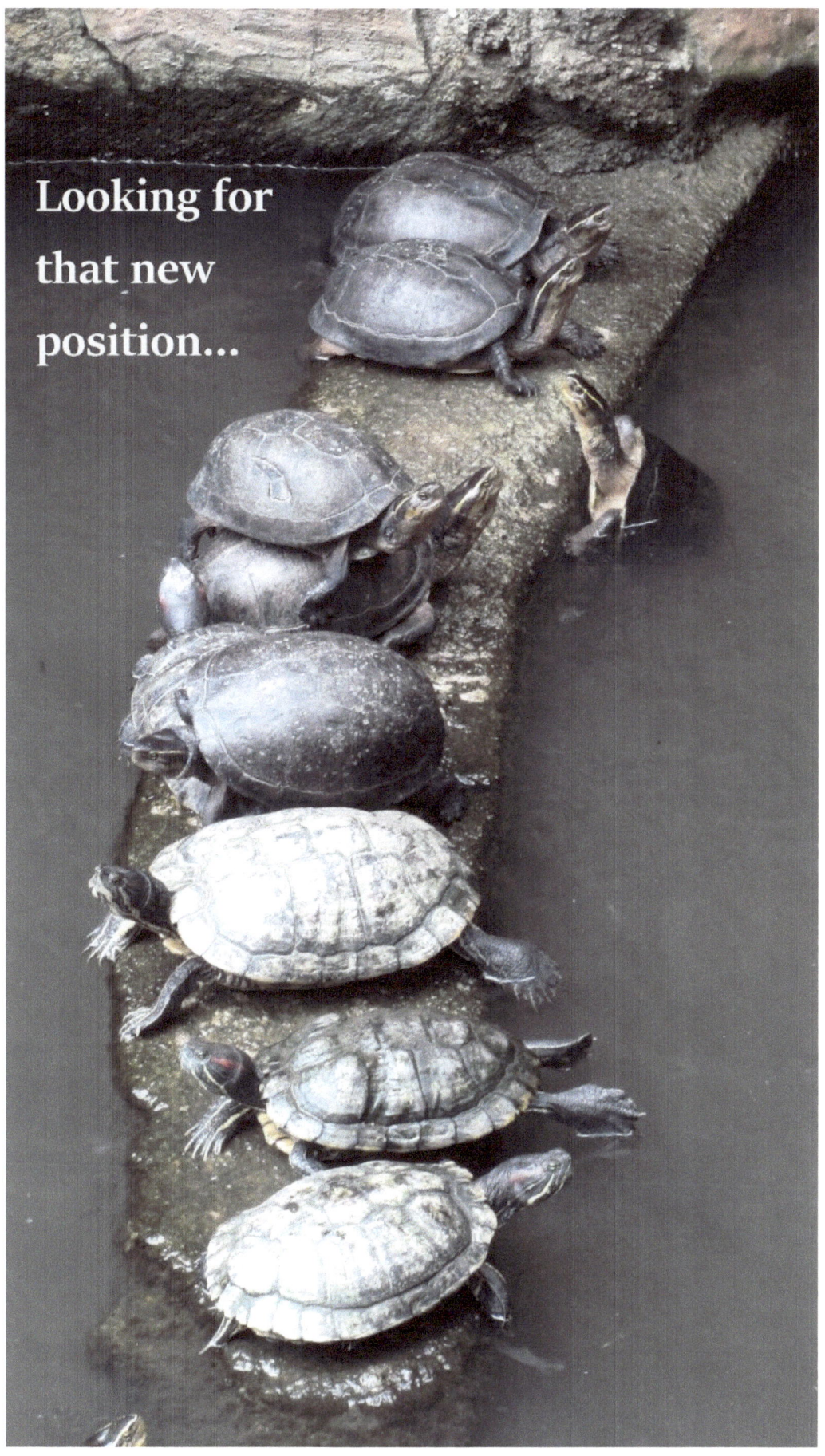

Looking for that new position...

**Between a rock
and a hard place...**

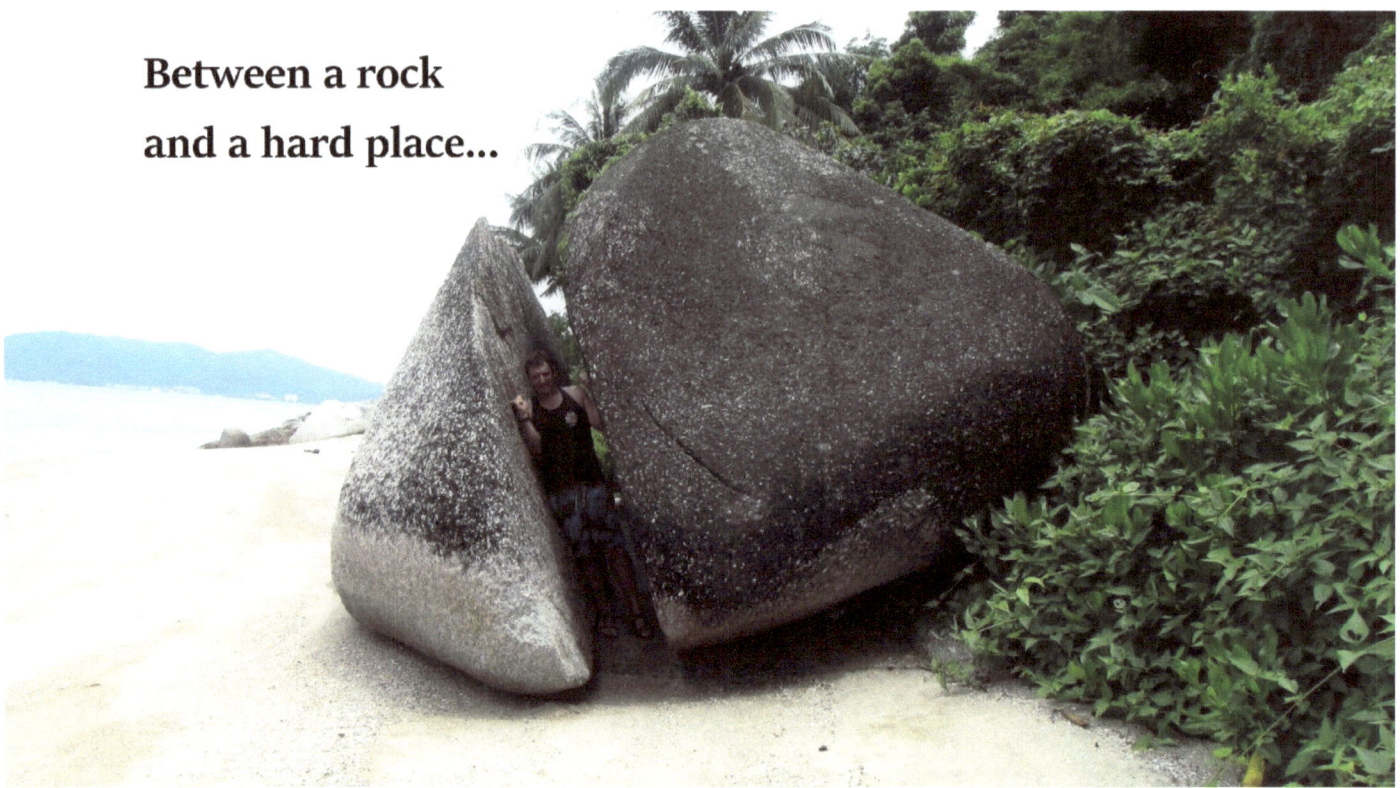

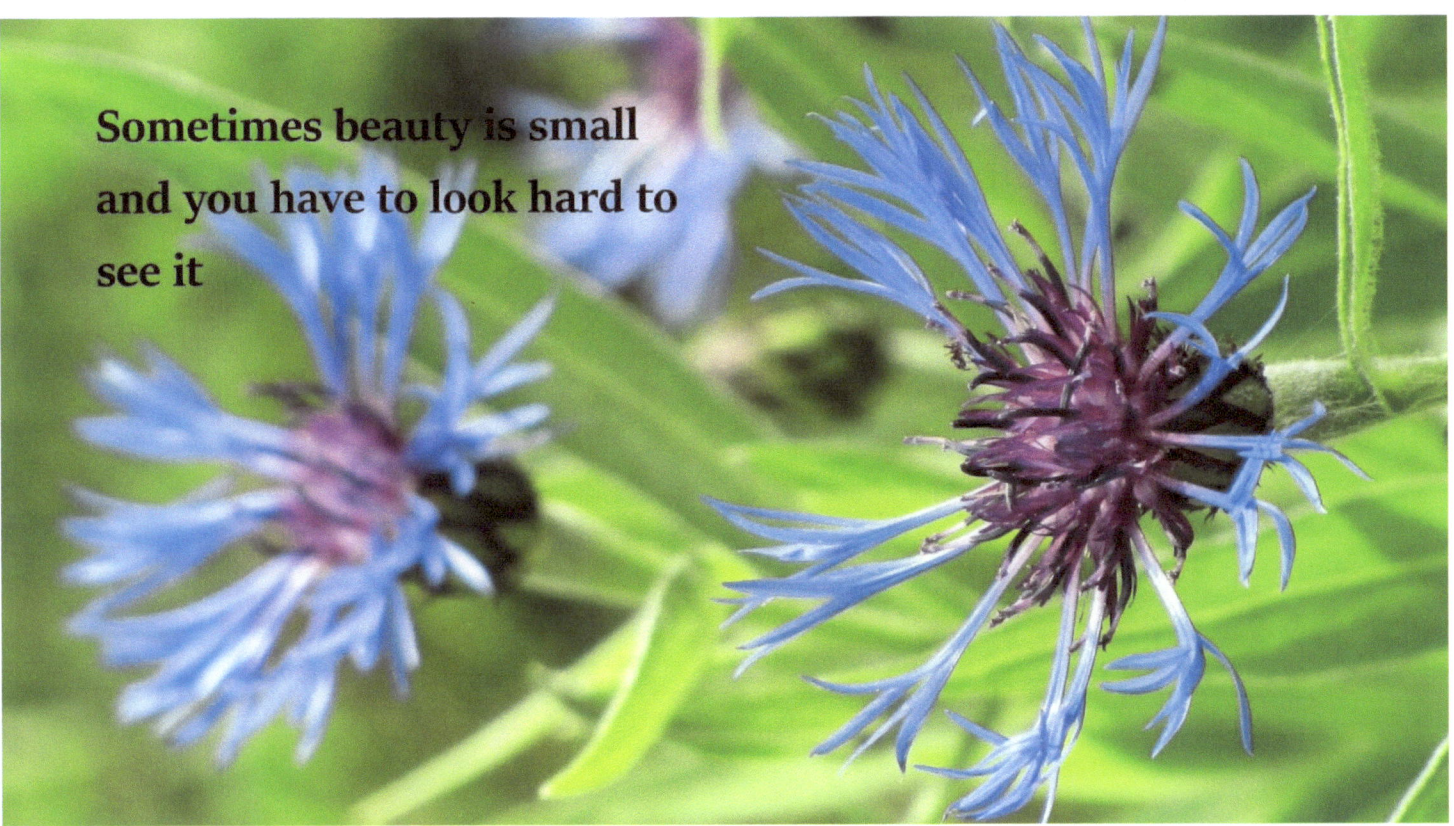

Sometimes beauty is small and you have to look hard to see it

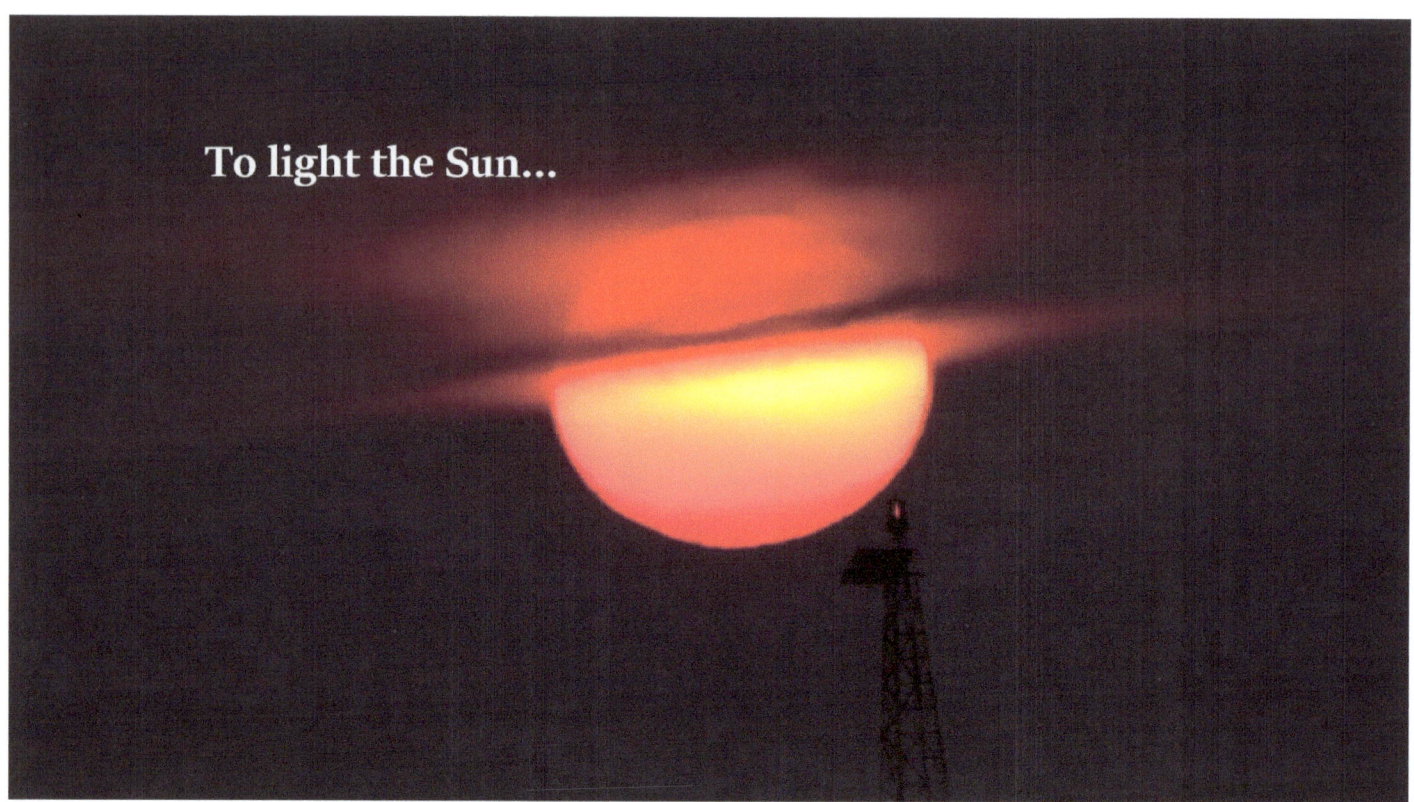

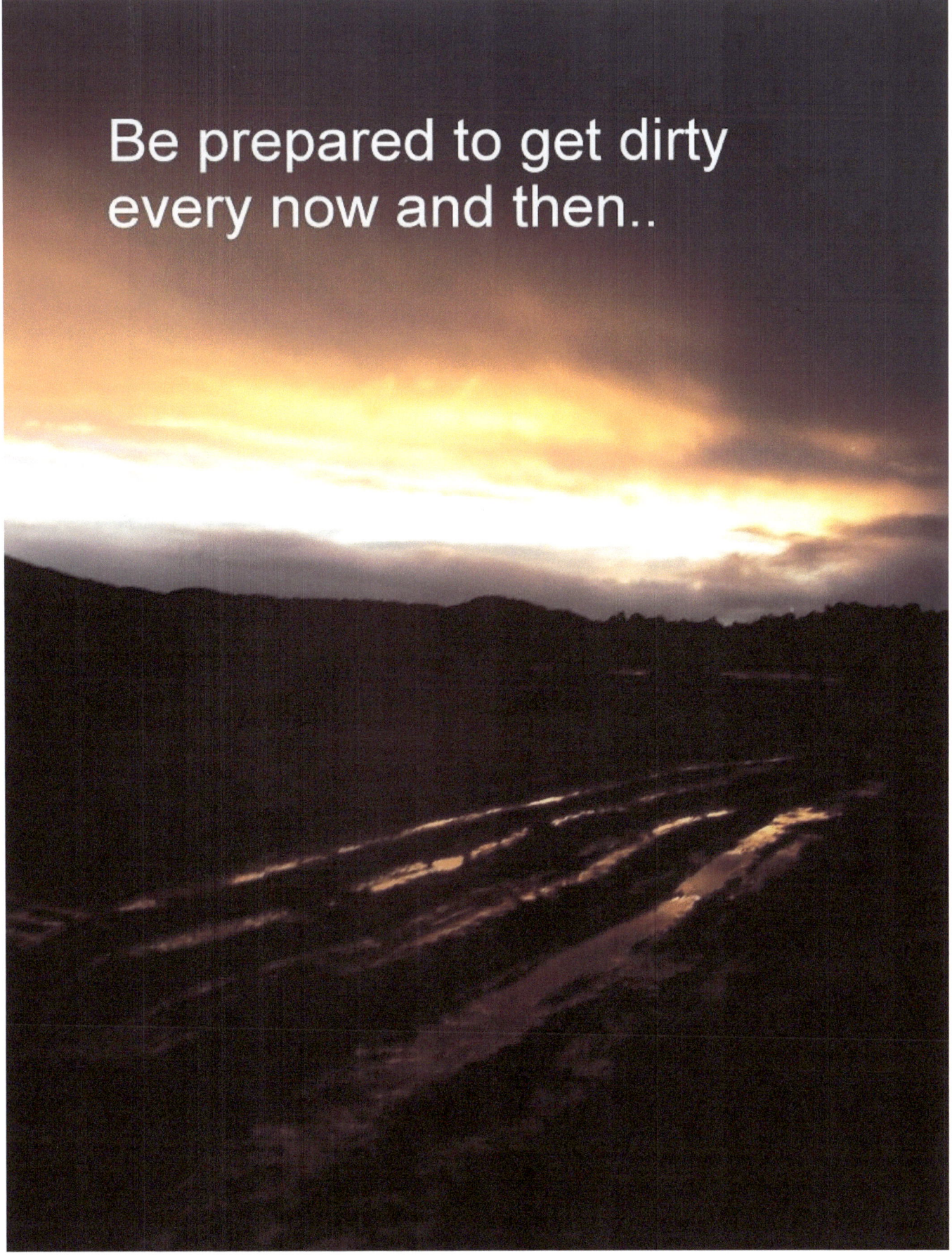

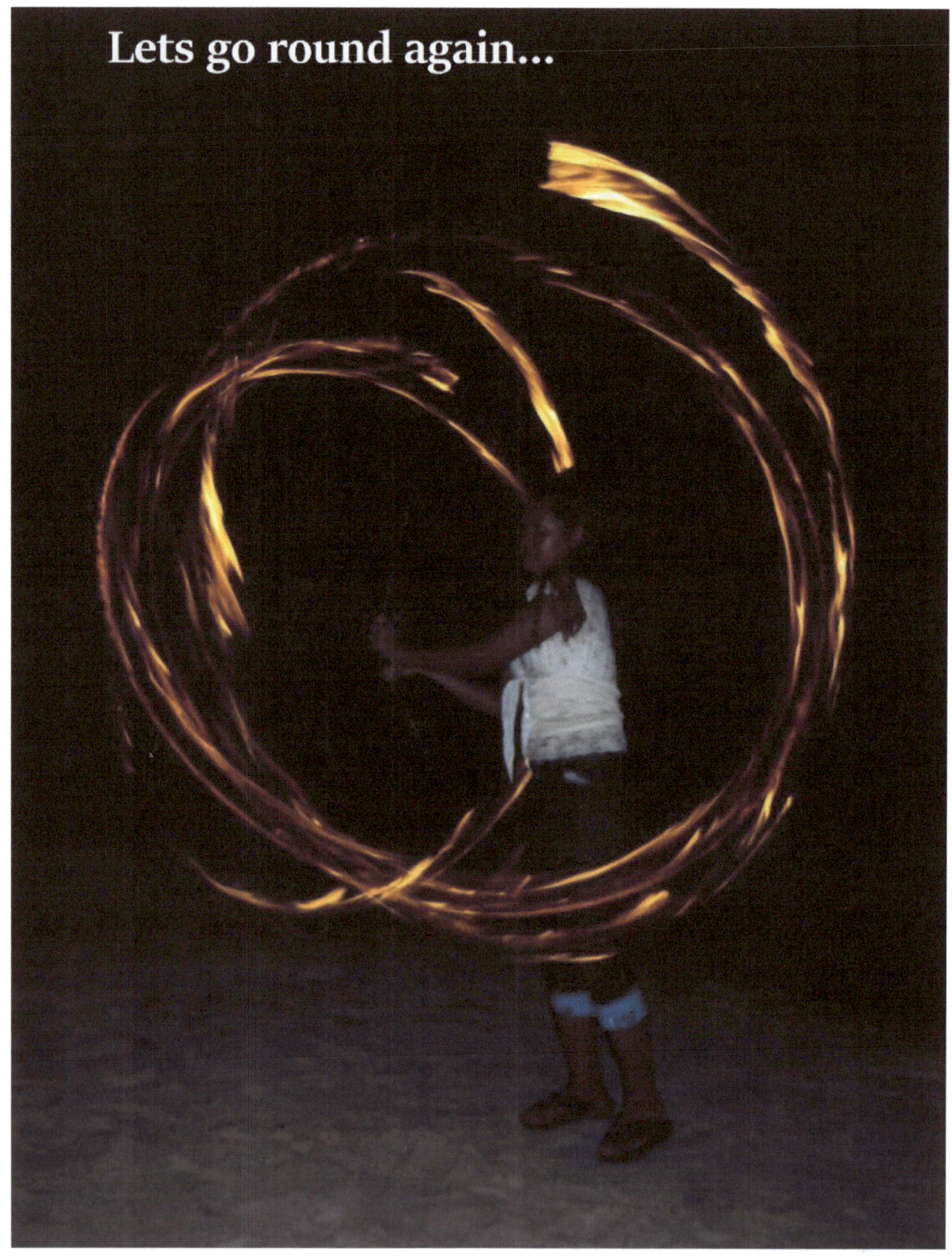

Lets go round again...

ABOUT THE AUTHOR

**David has a B.Sc. in Psychology and M.Sc's
in Ergonomics and Computing. Born in Northern Ireland
but currently residing in Bristol (U.K) and working in the
area of Ergonomics.**

www.ingramcontent.com/pod-product-compliance
Lightning Source LLC
Chambersburg PA
CBHW050726180526